Flipping Out

Why Every Business Should Be Franchise Ready

DOUG DOWNER

Flipping Out
Why Every Business Should Be Franchise Ready
Doug Downer

Disclaimer

This book is for educational purposes only. The author's intent is only to offer information of a general nature and based on their experiences working with business owners over more than 30 years. Professional advice should be sought before making any business decisions referred to within this book. In the event that you use any of the information in this book, the author and publisher assume no responsibility or liability for your actions.

ISBN: 9781792990496

<u>DEDICATION</u>

To the most important people in my life, Lisa, Taylor, and Jackson, who inspire me to be the best I can be, and for allowing me to do what I do and share myself with so many businesses and business owners.

CONTENTS

ACKNOWLEDGMENTS

There are many contributors to my life, both personally and professionally. These people have defined who I am as an individual, and as a business executive. This is my opportunity to recognise those who have been instrumental in shaping me and my career.

I believe at the core of every person are their values and what they stand for. These are shaped by the people we encounter throughout our lives, particularly in the early stages of our development.

From the age of 11 to 16, I was in The Boy's Brigade, an international, interdenominational, Christian youth organisation established in 1883. The reason I mention this is because of the influence and impact two individuals had on me in my time at The Boy's Brigade: John Morrison and Alex Parker. These two men instilled the values of the Boy's Brigade: Obedience, Reverence, Discipline, Self-Respect, and Character. The Motto of The Boy's Brigade is "Sure & Steadfast." Sure, meaning confident, secure, and with faith. Steadfast, meaning staunch, unwavering, and dependable.

It was not until I sat down to write this book, that I reflected on these values that were instilled in me at such a young age. I realise now that they've stayed with me at an unconscious level throughout my life.

In my working life, the following people have positively impacted the business person that I have become. Michael Tregurtha, who promoted me into management at McDonald's and whose management style I endeavoured to emulate throughout my career. In my 14 years at McDonald's, I was positively influenced and developed by five senior executives: Pete Ritchie, Charlie Bell, Guy Russo, Catriona Noble, and Mike Bolton; and by the thousands of Macca's team members and managers who I had the pleasure to work with.

There was a group of managers (George Sleiman, Andrew Iali, Michael Hansia, John MacPhail, and Michael Sleiman) who worked with me at McDonald's from 1988 to 1994. The best way to describe them and what they did for me is with the following quote:

"If I have seen further it is by standing on the shoulders of giants."

— Isaac Newton

We remain friends after 30 years. John went on to be the best business partner an owner could ask for, and Michael Sleiman has always been there for me in my current business with anything I needed, be it business, moral, or financial support. All of these guys have gone on to start and run their own successful businesses.

(Jeremy) James Fitzgerald gave me the opportunity to become a Director in the Foodco business, and taught me more about franchising and retail than any other individual in my career.

Peter and Deb Davis gave me the opportunity to step out of Retail franchising and into professional services franchising, They have been a huge support to me in the establishment of my current business, and continue to be there for me as my friends and mentors.

To all the franchisees and franchisors I have worked with, and to all of the business owners who have trusted me to work with them and be part of their teams—all of you have helped me and contributed to the content of this book and my business success.

I would like to thank the following people for their contribution to the book, to business in Australia, and for inspiring me to be better.

Peter Ritchie, Catriona Noble, Ray Itaoui, Steve Hansen, Peter Davis, Jason Zickerman, Peter Elligett, Wade Death, Pete Haselhurst, and Ankur Sehgal.

CHAPTER 1

MONEY BOTTLES, PAPER RUNS & FLIPPING BURGERS

The Foundations of Growth

"'I could be CEO of this company one day.' I realise that sounds arrogant [but] it really wasn't about me; it was about the company. The company and the people in it made me feel like anything was possible."

*— Catriona Noble,
Former MD & CEO McDonald's
Australia, Current MD Retail Distribution
ANZ MD & CEO*

THE FOUNDATIONS OF GROWTH

It was 1974 and I was already years ahead of the average eight year old, in that I identified how to make money from other people's waste. Today, we have the container deposit scheme recycling program where you get 10¢ per recyclable container.

Back then, 'money bottles' were worth 5¢ each when you returned them to the corner store, and this kept me going with mixed lollies, games on the pinball machine, and arcade games. By the time I was 10 years old, the value of returning these 'money bottles' increased to 20¢. Up until then, my process of collecting and returning 'money bottles' was a little haphazard, but I recognised that if I perfected my craft, I could make some really good money.

I identified my target audience by working out which units and households had a stronger demographic and were more likely to purchase the more expensive beverage bottles; those that had the recycling refund attached to them. I knew what days the bottles were put out and when they were picked up by the waste management company.

I had a lucrative little operation making between $3.00 and $5.00 a week. I controlled my area of Bondi, and I used to refer to myself as the 'Money Bottle King'.

But just like in any business, we encountered competition. There was another kid, Dominic P., and his two brothers who started working in my territory. What made it worse was that they lived in the adjoining suburb and were encroaching on my turf.

I had to react, so I enlisted the services of other local kids to be part of my team. I created schedules and ran my crew like a well-oiled drill team, and our operation and income grew.

I didn't realise at the time, but I was effectively acting like a franchisor. I had a system, processes, finance function, employees, and competitors. And I was effectively taking a royalty from the other kids on my team, as I would pay them 15¢ of the 20¢ I collected.

But nothing in business remains constant. The manufacturers changed their bottling from glass to plastic and the recycling of 'money bottles' declined, and so I had to find an alternative source of income.

Enter the best paperboy in the Eastern suburbs of Sydney, starting with newspaper deliveries Monday to Sunday mornings, and paper sales Friday afternoon and on the weekend, after I finished my deliveries. Not content with just one paper run, I would get up at 5.30am every morning and typically had two delivery runs, and I filled in when needed for additional runs if other kids failed to turn up.

I worked out which were the best streets in the suburb of Bondi in terms of the more affluent clientele. The reason this was important, was because of the tips I would generate from both deliveries and paper sales. Once I established the right target market, I set about delivering to them an experience that no other paper boy could match. I would leave flowers that I picked from gardens in the area for all my female customers.

For key events throughout the year, I would leave a card or small gift in the weeks leading up to things like Easter, Mother's Day, and Christmas.

Much to my chagrin, Dominic P. appeared on the scene as a paperboy. You could say he was my nemesis, but he was no match for my service and entrepreneurial activity.

I recognised very early on in my life the need for a systematic approach to business. If there were gold medals up for grabs for 8 to 12 year olds in the obscure business fields of recycling, newspaper sales, and delivery, then I was the Michael Phelps and Usain Bolt of that time in those industries.

I continued on as a paper boy until I was old enough to get a job at Grace Bros in the cheese department. I learnt to really enjoy cheese. My real love was going to the movies, so getting a role in the candy bar at Hoyts Bondi was ideal. All the Movies, Popcorn, Choc tops, and Coke you could consume were among the many perks.

But what I learnt at both of those places, was the discipline and processes involved in running operations in businesses of that size. Grace Bros had 163 stores and over 20,000 employees, while Hoyts had over 20 cinemas and more than 2000 employees. They had a formula that worked.

In 1983, at the age of 16, I moved out of home and needed a job that would be able to support me while I completed my last two years of High school and HSC. I found my home for the next 14 years at McDonald's.

I'm going to share some significant learnings and experiences from McDonald's with you throughout this book. The reason is simple: over 36,000 restaurants operating in 119 countries. There quite simply is no other company that emulates the success they have achieved.

How does a business get 15 and 16 year old kids to run multi-million dollar restaurants? As a parent, I can't even get my children to clean their room, pick up their clothes, or wash up a bowl they put in the sink—that is if they actually put the bowl in the sink!

The answer is complex yet simple—systems and processes.

In this book, you will hear from some of the greatest leaders of McDonald's in Australia, together with the experiences of other senior franchise executives who have gone on to develop and run very successful businesses. They did this using the foundations of what they learnt in their time in various franchise systems, and they will share with you the key learnings, which you can apply in your own business to assist you get your business franchise ready.

If you're reading this book, then you're most likely an aspiring business owner, an existing business owner who wants to grow their business, or someone who may have thought about franchising but didn't know where to start.

I wrote this book because I believe every business should be franchise ready. Not every business should or will become a franchise, but every business should be ready to franchise. This forces you to systemise and remove the dependency on you, the business owner, which enables a business to grow exponentially.

There's proof that systemised businesses, with documented processes operate successfully regardless of whether or not the owner is active, sell for a much greater value. While business valuation is important (we will always have to sell at some point), it is just as crucial that the business owner is able to remove themselves from doing 'everything' in the business.

Business owners go into business for a range of reasons: to be their own boss, to perfect their craft, to create a legacy, to hopefully have more money than they would make as an employee, to provide for their family, and for the pride of creating their own business and destiny. But the one I hear most is, to have freedom and quality of life.

If you speak to 99% of business owners, they will tell you that particularly in the early stages of a business's growth, they were or are the hardest working and lowest paid employees in their business.

There are over 134 Million results on Google regarding the stages of business growth, with anywhere from four to seven stages identified.

A significant proportion of business owners will have similar experiences in their journey. I believe business is a rollercoaster, with lots of ups and downs, which can be scary at times but exhilarating at others.

I have identified what I hold to be the eight stages of business growth and the associated ups and downs that go with each.

THE EIGHT STAGES OF BUSINESS GROWTH

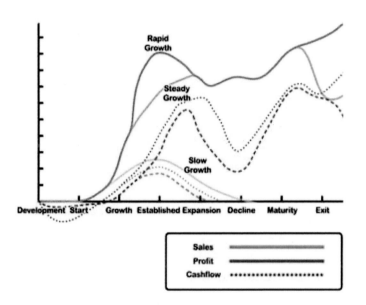

1. **Development**

   The Development phase is where the founder of the business has identified an idea, as either a concept or product, that they would like to take to market. At this stage the founder needs to complete the requisite research to determine if there is in fact a need for the proposed business. The creation of a well-structured business plan is essential. There is no positive cash flow and no profitability; only expenditure.

2. **Start-Up**

   The business is now a reality. You've registered the business entity, your products and services are in operation, and you have customers paying for your products and services.

   In this phase, business owners have a tendency to take on any customers and do whatever it takes to survive. The owners are working hard, primarily as technicians, and the business works because the owner is working so hard. The business succeeds and grows because of the efforts of the business owner.

   At this stage, the owner is fulfilling most functions in the business, with particular attention on marketing to grow the business, and finance to manage the cashflow.

   As entrepreneurs, we are typically optimistic and think things will happen quicker than they actually will. The start-up phase can be frustrating. It can take a long time for businesses to move through the next stages of their growth. There are sales but not as many controls in place, so cash flow is good, but profitability is low. The owner is probably not taking a nominal salary, if any at all.

3. **Growth**

   There are three types of growth that you may experience: slow growth, steady growth, or rapid growth.

   Slow growth can be challenging, especially after all the hard work that you've put into the business. Globally, 50% of all start-up businesses close their doors within the first five years, as they don't grow at the rate they need to sustain their operating costs.

Achieving *steady growth* enables the owner to fine tune operations and perfect their business model.

Rapid growth sounds great, but can be just as challenging as slow growth, as it requires the business owner to be involved with more activity. In most cases, the owner hasn't been able to add the right resources to the business and is often still completing most tasks themselves. In this case, they are unable to bring in the right people to delegate responsibility to. Periods of rapid growth may see significantly greater cash flow but lower profitability, because the systems and processes are not in place to manage the extra demands of a fast growing business.

4. Established

The Established phase sees stability within the business, with consistent sales and strong customer loyalty. The business owner has time to focus on strategy and developing the next stage in the development of the business.

Sales are still growing but not as rapidly, and profitability is strong. At this stage, the business owner can start to realise their desire for freedom and quality of life.

It's important that the owner does not take their foot off the accelerator too much. This can happen as the business operations becomes more routine.

The business needs to continue to invest into human resources and bring in additional expertise. It's time to ensure that policies and procedures that got the business to this stage are documented to enable scale and expansion.

It's in the established phase that the business owner needs to determine what's next. Should they expand? If so, how should they do it?

This is normally when a business owner should consider franchising.

5. Expansion

This stage is characterised by growth either into new markets or distribution channels.

Moving into new markets includes opening in new locations, while distribution channels may include either, or both, vertical and horizontal integration. Vertical integration includes taking control of the supply chain and generating additional income, while maintaining quality and control over key products, supplies, and ingredients. Horizontal integration includes the acquisition of similar-type companies that can be bolted onto the existing business.

In the expansion stage, business owners will consider a range of vehicles to achieve continued growth, and the concept of franchising can be used to expand.

It is important to know that expanding into any new product will see an increase in sales and cash flow, but will have a significant impact on profitability, as investment is made in areas unfamiliar to the business owner. In most cases, this will take the business back into the start-up stage.

6. Decline

Business is increasingly more competitive, and if owners don't reinvigorate their business and brands, or if they take their eye of their core business and get too distracted by growth for growth's sake, their core business has the potential to go into decline.

Every business has to reinvent themselves and ensure that

their leadership is keeping in touch with the changing marketplace. One only has to look at the carnage in the Australian and international retail landscape to see the huge decline in business performance.

Going into decline is not necessarily the death nail for a business. Most will experience a decline in sales, market share, and profitability over time. It's how they react to the decline that determines the success of the business and its ability to progress to the maturity stage of growth. Just look at McDonald's and how they had to reinvent themselves in the past 15 years with advent of McCafé, salads, healthy options, and the introduction of a totally different service style. This includes kiosk operations and a huge increase in the number of products sold, entry into the gourmet market, dining room upgrades, and store remodels. It's a dramatically different business to the one I worked in for so long, but reinvention was required to address stiffer competition and declining sales and relevance.

7. Maturity

The growth and expansion stages bring about diversification, but this can at times create challenges as the business is not fully matured. The maturity stage sees business sales steadily growing while delivering consistent and strong profitability. It's the period where businesses will spend the greatest amount of time.

Diversification and developing new products and markets is critical, as competition will be more significant.

8. Exit

At some stage in the life of a business, the founder or owner will exit the business, and this can be done a number of ways. It is the opportunity for the owner to cash out on all the effort and years of hard work.

In some cases, business owners may elect to shut down their business, I find this happens when the business has not adequately developed its systems and reinvented itself.

The key to exiting a business is a realistic valuation. It may have been years of hard work to build the company, but think about the real value in the current marketplace.

Each stage of the business growth cycle might not occur in chronological order. Some businesses will be 'built to flip', quickly going from start-up to exit. Others will choose to avoid expansion, and stay in the established staged, as it provides the life the owner desires. The reality is that no one lives for forever. But hopefully the business the owner/founder has created will live on beyond their generation, with realised value they can take from it.

Due to a lack of planning, a majority of business owners are faced with the harsh reality that their business is not worth what they think it is, when it's time to exit their business.

96% of business owners agree that having an exit strategy is important

Only 12% of business owners have an exit strategy!

75% of business owners who sold their business had post-exit remorse

This book is written for every business owner who is currently working hard in their business and wants to take it to the next level. This book will show you how others have scaled to ensure that they have a better business and a better life. So, when it finally comes time to sell or exit your business, you can yield the benefits of all your hard work.

If the idea of being a franchisor doesn't appeal to you, I want you to think about this book and the concept of franchising from two perspectives.

1. An External Franchise
2. An Internal Franchise

An external franchise is what we you may currently be familiar with. It's businesses like the McDonald's, Subway, Jim's Group, Poolwerx, and 7-Eleven.

An internal franchise utilises all of the same principles of the traditional franchise model, but instead of franchisees, it requires the treatment of your employees as if they were the franchisees. This creates an ownership mindset, which is one of the benefits of franchising.

If anyone has ever asked you "Are you a franchise?" then you should think about it.

Being a franchisor is not for everyone, but thinking and behaving like a franchisor is a must for every business.

Takeaways

- ❖ Systems and processes are the key for businesses to grow.

- ❖ Start thinking and acting like a franchisor even if you don't intend to franchise.

- ❖ Understand the different stages of business growth and what each stage will do with regards to profitability and cash flow.

- ❖ Think about your exit strategy now and start planning for it from the outset.

- ❖ Think about who your likely buyer might be.

CHAPTER 2

IT'S NOT A BUSINESS,,
IT'S A WAY OF DOING BUSINESS

What Is Franchising?

"With a franchise, you have someone who cares as much about the business name and image as you do because they own it "

—Jim Evanger

WHAT IS FRANCHISING?

Have you ever heard the term 'disenfranchised' and wondered what it meant? Every time I hear that someone is disenfranchised, I cringe. It is used out of context and relates to a feeling of disappointment that someone may have with their circumstances, or a reaction to something they are experiencing.

It's at this time it makes me think about what a franchise is.

To be disenfranchised means to have your legal rights taken away from you. Therefore, to have a franchise means the granting of legal rights. In the case of business, it means the right to use intellectual property that has been developed by an individual through a company. That company can license the rights for an individual or entity to use the system that they have developed.

The concept of franchising is not new. It's been around since the middle ages when the government gave licenses to churches and local council to collect taxes, and for medieval lords to grant rights to individuals to sell their wares and produce.

In 1731, when Benjamin Franklin expanded his print shop business and newspaper production to additional locations, he granted the rights for individuals to use the systems and processes that he had developed and perfected. In so doing, he charged them a fee for these rights.

There are three modern day franchising heroes: Isaac Singer, Henry Ford, and Ray Kroc.

Isaac Singer, the inventor of the Singer sewing machine, was a pioneer of modern day franchising. At the time, most sewing was done by hand. A Singer sewing machine had a significantly greater capacity but one huge limitation—the cost. Singer's response was to offer customers the option to pay for the machine in instalments. This created huge demand for the product, but Singer now needed a better system of distribution and servicing. His solution was to recruit business people who would pay him an upfront license (franchise) fee for the territorial rights to sell the sewing machines, and to provide the ongoing service to the customers in the territories where the machines were sold.

Around the same time, Henry Ford was starting to mass produce motor vehicles. His method of sale was through travelling salesmen, which proved to be unprofitable. So, he licensed two car dealerships, and the Ford motor company franchise model was born.

And then there's my personal favourite, Ray Kroc. Ray was not the founder of McDonald's, nor did he come up with the idea of franchising McDonald's. But he certainly perfected it.

Ray was a multi-mixer (milkshake maker) salesman who went door-to-door selling multi-mixer machines. The significance of this piece of machinery was that each machine made five milkshakes at once, and the founders of McDonald's, Dick and Maurice the McDonald brothers, has just put in an order for eight machines. Ray was fascinated and wanted to see why they had made such an order.

After observing their operation, Ray envisaged the McDonald's system being rolled out right across America. Ray couldn't sleep that night with his excitement about the opportunity that the McDonald's business represented.

> *"When I saw it working that day in 1954, I felt like some latter-day Newton who'd just had an Idaho potato caromed off his skull. That night in my motel room I did a lot of heavy thinking about what I'd seen during the day. Visions of McDonald's restaurants dotting crossroads all over the country paraded through my brain."*

> **—Ray Kroc**

Much to Ray's delight, the McDonald's brothers were looking for an agent to sell franchises across the country. With Ray's 30 years in sales, he was in the right place at the right time.

> *"The two most important requirements for major success are: first, being in the right place at the right time, and second, doing something about it."*

> **—Ray Kroc**

Ray cemented a deal to be the McDonald brothers' exclusive agent and started selling franchises. Ray tried to convince the brothers that they should start thinking bigger and continue to expand the business, but the McDonald's brothers were content. They started to put the brakes on with Ray and his vision of growing the brand.

Ray ended up buying out the McDonald brothers for $2.7 million after learning that they weren't as motivated as he was in building a restaurant empire.

> *"The McDonald brothers were simply not on my wavelength at all. I was obsessed with the idea of making McDonald's the biggest and the best. They were content with what they had; they didn't want to be bothered with more risks and more demands."*
>
> **—Ray Kroc**

As you can see, franchising is not a business but a way of leveraging the systems, processes, and intellectual property that has been developed and perfected to ensure a smoother transition into a business. Ray Kroc didn't invent it, but he took it more seriously than anyone else.

> *"We take the hamburger business more seriously than anyone else."*
>
> **—Ray Kroc**

THERE ARE THREE TYPES OF FRANCHISE MODELS

Manufacturing franchises: used by organisations such as Coca-Cola where a license is issued to another party to make their product.

Coca-Cola's franchising system dates back to 1889 when bottling rights began to be sold to businessmen who were capable of large-scale bottling, and thus were able to quickly expand the product into new markets. One of the early 'brand standards' set for the system was an agreement by the bottlers to only sell the product in a standard and unique 'contour' bottle, patented in 1915. These were in fact one type 'money bottles' I used to collect and return for recycling payment back in the 1970s.

The Coca-Cola Company produces syrup concentrate, then sells it to bottlers around the world, who hold an exclusive territory to bottle and sell the end product. These bottling partners manufacture, package, and distribute the finished product to vending partners, who then sell directly to consumers.

Product franchises: used by organisations such as Ford Motor car, who issue them to dealers to sell their cars.

Or as we have seen more recently, movie and television 'franchises' follow a formula and are owned by a group that licenses the rights to produce and screen the productions.

Almost every professional sporting competition in the world includes franchises, where sporting teams are granted the license to operate within a geographical territory. This has been very common in the USA, with baseball franchises being granted in 1876 and every NFL Gridiron team, NHL hockey team, or NBL Basketball team operating a franchise issued by their governing body.

Business format franchising: this is the most common form of franchising, where a highly recognised and branded outlet is franchised to a franchisee for them to operate under strict conditions for a fixed term.

Familiar brands that use a business format franchise approach include the majority of the bricks and mortar operations, like McDonald's and KFC.

Current Day Franchising

We have experienced some turbulent times with franchising in Australia with parliamentary enquiries into the sector. It seems to see negative press on a weekly basis, but these challenges are not exclusive to Australia, with similar challenges globally. The thing is, the stories are headline grabbing and often one sided.

The problem is not franchising per se, but a minority of individuals who happen to be in some high profile franchise organisations. They have done the wrong thing, and this is causing aspersions to be cast on the franchise sector as a whole.

The process of franchising is sound but it's important to understand that **franchising is not a business—it's a way of doing business.**

People have been doing business since the beginning of time. According to Rudyard Kipling, prostitution was 'the world's oldest profession', when in fact there are a number of industries and professions that emerged well before prostitution. These included builders, farmers, musicians, artists, story tellers, clothiers, tailors, hunters, butchers, and toolmakers. Why do I mention these professions? Because all of them have been franchised in modern times. Every business has the potential to be scaled, and most businesses have the potential to be licensed or franchised.

It's important to understand a little more about what franchising is other than its origins or the core principles of it being a license to use the systems and processes of a developed brand.

Marketing Strategy

Franchising is a business strategy for getting and keeping customers. It is a marketing system for creating an image in the minds of current and future customers, of how the company's products and services can help them. It is a method for distributing products and services that satisfy customers' needs.

Interdependence

Franchising requires interdependence, where both the franchisee and franchisor have needs to be met.

Interdependence is working within the confines of the requirements of the franchisor, for the mutual benefit and consistency of all other franchisees within that system. There is also a dependence on the franchisor to provide leadership, development of the brand, and support of the franchisees.

Dependence is part of any franchise relationship, as the franchisee relies on the franchisor to guide them towards success. But the system alone will not guarantee success. It is up to each franchisee to make the system work for them, and in turn they need to work for, and within, the system.

Independence is ignoring others and any coexistence, wanting to deal with everything alone, and not acknowledging any need for support. Often, franchisors are largely independent operators who want to run their own show. Independent individuals make good franchisors, but not necessarily good franchisees.

Franchising is a network of interdependent business relationships that allows a number of people to share:

o   A brand identity
o   A successful method of doing business
o   A proven marketing and distribution system
o   A product or service that is differentiated from the competition

In short, franchising is a strategic alliance between groups of people who have specific relationships and responsibilities, with a common goal to dominate the markets that they operate within.

There are many misconceptions about franchising, but probably the most widely held is that a franchisee is 'buying a franchise'. In reality, the franchisee is investing their assets in a system to utilise the brand name, operating system, and ongoing support. Every franchisee in the system is licensed to do this.

If a franchisee was in fact 'buying a franchise', they would most likely feel entitled to operate the business the way they would like, and would make entrepreneurial decisions about their business that may contradict how the franchisor needs the business to be run.

The key to the success of any franchise system starts with the premise that the franchisor does not sell franchises; they grant the rights for individuals to use the intellectual property of the brand.

<u>Takeaways</u>

- ❖ Franchising is not a business. It's a way of doing business.

- ❖ Determine if franchising is the right business model for you to grow your business.

- ❖ Nearly every business can be franchised.

- ❖ Every business can adopt the principles of a franchised business.

- ❖ Franchising is a marketing process.

- ❖ Franchisees don't 'buy' a franchise. They are granted the rights to use and leverage the intellectual property of a brand.

CHAPTER 3

SELF-EMPLOYED OR BUSINESS OWNER

Why Should You Be Franchise Ready?

"If your business depends on you, you don't own a business, you have a job. And it's the worst job in the world because you're working for a lunatic!"

—Michael E Gerber

Why Should You Be Franchise Ready?

Business owners are crazy. The risk is enormous, we live in uncertain times with an economy and government that makes it difficult for businesses to succeed, financing has become increasingly more difficult, competition is everywhere, and the multinationals have an unfair advantage in scaling their businesses.

As business owners, we put everything on the line.

Despite the deck being stacked against them, entrepreneurs create new businesses every day.

So what actually makes a business owner successful?

"It's about having a system and processes for making business easier and less dependent on the Business Owner."

-   ***Doug Downer***

Success is in the eye of the individual, or the entrepreneur, who makes the decision to leave the safety and sanity of paid employment to become self-employed.

There are three main reasons employees leave employment:
- Retirement
- Disability, inability, or lack of desire to work
- Self-employment

"Every Business Owner is Self-Employed but not every Self-Employed person is a Business Owner."

—Doug Downer

You may have been wondering if there are any actual differences between being Self-Employed and being a Business owner.

What Is the Difference?

Early on in the development of a business, the differences are minute, but as the business develops the differences become stark.

Time and Money

Self-employed don't have the luxury of time like the established business owner.

The self-employed entrepreneur is essentially exchanging time for money, and if they're not working, they're not making money. So, they tend to keep themselves busy as often as possible and their focus is on immediate income.

The self-employed entrepreneur typically doesn't have any employees, so they end up doing everything themselves: marketing, accounts, tax, sales, and administration. Often, their passion is actually the technical aspects of their venture.

These tasks take them away from their core, and in most cases their productivity is not as good as a dedicated professional in that space. A good entrepreneur will outsource these functions, enabling them to focus on their core expertise and often what they enjoy.

The business owner is more concerned with lifestyle and work/life integration, wealth creation, and building an asset, because the business has employed individuals to help the business grow.

Work/Life Balance Is a Furphy

I refer to the term work/life integration rather than work/life balance. The reason is that employees have work/life balance, but business owners and the self-employed need to integrate their work into their life. In most cases it *is* their life, particularly when the business starts and is in the early stages of development. I would like to reiterate the misnomer that going into business will somehow give the business owner a better quality of life. It will eventually, but it will take some time. Be prepared to work hard and put systems in place to remove the dependence on the owner.

The Gerber Effect

The self-employed works in the business, while the business owner works on it.

The self-employed are responsible for all of the income generating activities, and they apply their trade and the technical aspects of their skillset and passion. They are the technician.

The established business owner is focused on the strategic activities and building an enterprise that has structure, systems, and processes, so it can be scaled to grow and work without them.

Michael Gerber immortalised the concept in his book *The E-Myth*, detailing the technician starting a business without the requisite skills to grow a business. They have this propensity to remain a technician working in the business doing the-day to-day, rather than strategically thinking and acting in a way that has them focus on the business.

Autopilot

The business owner's business runs on autopilot while that of the self-employed doesn't.

One of the ways that owners have learnt to build a business, is to make it run on autopilot. This means that they are poised to create processes and systems that would help the business run irrespective of whether the business owner was present or not. This might not be the same case with the self-employed, as an absence in the field of business may cause a plummet in sales.

The Role of the Business Owner

A business owner focuses on building both tangible and intangibles assets, by developing goodwill in the their business and brand.

A business owner is seeking returns. The primary focus for many self-employed people is selling their time and skills. Business owners, by contrast, are looking for much more than a wage: they are seeking a return on their investment commensurate with the capital, skill, and time they have invested in it.

There is no right or wrong when it comes to deciding whether to be a business owner or simply self-employed.

Either way, both can prepare their operations to mirror that of a franchise operation that will deliver systems and processes, and improved operations, sales, and profitability.

Case Study

I worked with a very successful self-employed operator (let's call him Steve) who had been operating his marketing 'business' for over 20 years. It was a substantial business turning over in excess of $650,000 and was extremely profitable. But he was the only person in the 'business'. He did everything himself, which kept him exceptionally busy but also meant his 'business' was a bit lumpy in terms of sales. When he had a lot of work, he wasn't focused on marketing and lead generation, so he would have a great month followed by a lean month. This cycle created further challenges for him when it came to taking time away from the business, and at the end of the financial and calendar year when budgets were tight.

Steve was over 60 years of age and as we started working together, I was trying to get him to plan for his retirement. I tried to convince Steve that he needed to scale and start to employ people into his operation. This would make the business less dependent on him and give us the opportunity to turn his enterprise into a business that he could sell. Steve didn't want to manage staff, and he was comfortable with the idea that his enterprise would not be worth as much when he decided to retire, so he could 'just take his shingle down' and close up the business.

So, rather than force him to become a business and employ staff, we set about building a strategy and plan to systemise his operation. By engaging sub-contractors who could do some of the work for him, we were able to iron out the fluctuations in sales and give Steve some time to himself. This enabled him to enjoy life outside of his 'business'. Steve will be able to realise some of the equity he built up over the previous 20 years of operation when it comes time to exit and sell.

Why Someone Should Consider Being a Franchisor

There are a number of reasons *why* a business owner should consider becoming a franchisor.

Reliable Customer Experience

The success of so many businesses is linked to the proprietor and the love they have for their business and customers. It is difficult to have employees treat customers the same way that a business owner would. The best way to do this requires a systematic approach. This starts with who you recruit, how you onboard and train them, and the systems and processes that you document on the way you want things done. Franchising with the right owner/operator using your systems and processes correctly ensures consistency in the customer's experience.

People

It doesn't matter what product you sell, you're in the people business. When a business starts out, it's difficult for the owner to afford the perfect number and quality of people they need. So, systemising the business and looking to grow requires the recruitment of the right people. Franchising enables the business owner to bring likeminded individuals into the business as business partners/franchisees, who will for the most part deliver a better output than employees. These business owners/franchisees are a far higher calibre individuals than a business owner could afford to recruit for a company operated business.

Scale and Grow

Franchising enables the owner to scale and grow the business much quicker, than if they were to continue operating the business themselves. Starting to document the systems and processes of the business makes the business model stronger and easier to scale and grow.

Capital

Most entrepreneurs are bootstrapping when they start their business and have limited access to capital to fund growth. The funds that can be generated through franchising and franchise fees and ongoing royalties, can provide additional capital to grow and also make the business more attractive to banking institutions and investors.

Money

Scaling your business generates significantly more cashflow, albeit profitability typically declines in the early stages of establishing a franchise system. I have worked in four franchise systems with founders who told me they made more money before they decided to scale and grow. So, be ready for that, but it does get easier and better as you see more money flowing into your business.

'Passactive'

This is a phrase that I have coined. It is the combination of passive + active income = passactive. Franchising generates passive income for the franchisor, but in order to do so, the franchisor must be active in their operation and development of the business. If you're active, you'll generate passive income through royalties and product supply.

Time

This is most precious commodity known to mankind. It doesn't matter who you are, we all have the same amount of time each day to do what needs to be done. Franchising gives the owner the ability to grow quicker, and once the business has been scaled, it should provide more time to enjoy the fruits of their labour. But it needs to be said the emerging franchisor will work ridiculously long hours, until the business gets to a size where the business can recruit the resources it needs for the founder/owner to take a step back.

Exit

Having a business that operates without the founder/owner of the business makes it more attractive for potential purchasers, and easier for the founder to step back or exit.

Having profitable company-operated units does significantly increase the value of a business when it comes time to sell, because all of the profit is factored into the EBITDA, not just the royalties and franchise fees. But it does cost significantly more to establish the company operations. Having a mix of both operations is a good methodology, and this is best exemplified by Australian burger chain Grill'd. They will open company stores, as they are very profitable, and it enables them to be super selective with franchisees.

The table below best illustrates the impact of franchised operations and company operations, and you see the EBITDA and valuation with an increased number of company operated units.

Franchise Stores	Jun-19	Jun-20	Jun-21	Jun-22	Jun-23
Store Sales	2,000	2,000	2,000	2,000	2,000
Number of Stores	10	15	20	25	30
Store Revenue	20,000	30,000	40,000	50,000	60,000
Royalty	7.0%	7.0%	7.0%	7.0%	7.0%
Marketing	2.0%	2.0%	2.0%	2.0%	2.0%
Other	1.0%	1.0%	1.0%	1.0%	1.0%
Total Franchise Fee	10.0%	10.0%	10.0%	10.0%	10.0%
Initial Fee Revenue	50	250	250	250	250
Franchisor Revenue	2,000	3,250	4,250	5,250	6,250
Owned Stores	Jun-19	Jun-20	Jun-21	Jun-22	Jun-23
Store Sales	2,000	2,000	2,000	2,000	2,000
Number of Stores	4.0	6.0	8.0	10.0	12.0
Owned Store Revenue	8,000	12,000	16,000	20,000	24,000
Growth		50.0%	33.3%	25.0%	20.0%
COGS	(2,400)	(3,000)	(4,000)	(5,000)	(6,000)
Gross Profit	5,600	9,000	12,000	15,000	18,000
Gross Margin	70.0%	75.0%	75.0%	75.0%	75.0%
Store Margin	15.0%	15.0%	15.0%	15.0%	15.0%
EBITDA	1,200	1,800	2,400	3,000	3,600

It is commonly accepted that franchise businesses sell for a greater premium than independent businesses, because of their scalability and systemisation. However, the potential buyers for your business may be limited if they don't understand franchising, because it is a unique way of doing business.

The best examples of this in Australia are brands like Boost Juice, which sold in 2010 valued at $100 million at an EBITDA multiple of over 16 times, and was sold again in 2014 valued at approximately $185 million at an EBITDA multiple over 9 times.

Crust Pizza sold to Retail Food Group for an upfront payment of $41 million at an EBITDA of over 7 times.

Burger chain Grill'd is valued at somewhere between $237 million and $314 million.

Oporto and Red Rooster sold to Archer Capital for a reported $450 million at an EBITDA of over 13 times.

So, you can see from historical sales that established franchise groups can sell for multiples ranging between 7 to 16 times EBITDA, mirroring some highly successful tech businesses. This is significant when compared to the traditional business sales multiples that range from 2 to 5 times.

In the table on the following page, we have provided EBITDA multiples for Australian businesses within the retail and hospitality sector as these two sectors represent over 45% of the total franchise numbers in Australia.

Australian Businesses

The table below illustrates the range of business valuation multiples for all businesses within the retail and hospitality sectors in Australia.

EBITDA	Retail			Hospitality		
	Low	Mid	High	Low	Mid	High
Micro ($0–500K)	0.58	1.92	5.62	0.76	1.66	3.97
Small ($500k – $1m)	0.72	1.86	4.97	0.74	1.95	4.71
Medium ($1m – $5m)	0.97	2.17	4.93	0.99	2.29	4.59
Middle ($5m – $15m)	1.39	2.44	4.03	2.32	2.87	3.67

You will have noticed with the examples presented regarding the sale and acquisition of large Australian franchisor groups, that they have typically commanded much higher multiples than the whole industry. The reasons for this are not solely linked to EBITDA and tangible assets, as there are some intangible assets that come into play, including:

- The brand, marketing presence, and the investment made to date.
- The systems and processes that have been developed, better known as the intellectual property.
- Perfecting the model and the lessons learnt from the mistakes that have been made in establishing the franchise business.
- A proven and profitable business model.
- The human resources and expertise within a franchise business.

All of the attributes of a franchisor can be achieved by an independent business, so it's not critical to become a franchisor if the business owner has no desire to venture down that path.

"Run your business as if you're going to sell it. At some point you will sell it, so start planning now"

—Doug Downer

<u>Takeaways</u>

❖ Having documented systems and processes makes business easier and scalable.

❖ Every business owner is self-employed, but not every self-employed person is a business owner.

❖ Business owners make more money and have a better quality of life than the self-employed.

❖ Franchise businesses and systems sell for a significantly greater multiple than independent businesses, particularly if they have profitable company operations.

CHAPTER 4

HAMBURGER UNIVERSITY

What I Learnt from McDonald's

"If it's flipping hamburgers at McDonald's, be the best hamburger flipper in the world. Whatever it is you do you have to master your craft."

—Snoop Dogg

What I Learnt from McDonald's

As a kid growing up I used to enjoy going to McDonald's, but it was a rare experience and a real treat as we didn't have a lot of money. Even though I could only ever have a cheeseburger and had to share my fries and drink with my brother, I loved going to 'Maccas'. But I could never understand why kids would throw their pickles on the walls and ceiling, as that to me was the best part of the burger.

As much as I loved going to McDonald's, I never envisioned that I would ever work there. In fact, at one point I clearly stated to a couple of my mates, "There's no way I would ever work at McDonald's, what a dead-end job."

Fast forward forty years and I couldn't have been more wrong. I owe everything I have to my time at McDonald's. The friends that I made have lasted a lifetime, I met my wife Lisa in 1984 and we've been together ever since, and McDonald's built the foundation of my business principles, work ethic, and how to make a business and system work.

It was August 11, 2014 and I was sitting in a classroom in Denver Colorado. It was the beginning of an eight day, intensive business coach training course, and everyone had to get up at the front of the class to speak for three-to-five minutes about themselves and their background. This included why they were qualified to advise and support business owners.

I don't know if it was nerves or just the way they organised each of the participants to come out front and present themselves to the group, but going last made me even more anxious. Particularly after listening to the calibre of all the other participants and their business experience, qualifications, and university educations.

A large proportion of the students on my training course were international students, with a majority from Germany and the USA where university is a rite of passage. In Australia only 36% of students go on to University, while in the USA 70% of students go on to university.

In this particular class, every other participant went to university and had a degree to compliment there already impressive resume. Their speeches were about their alma mater and qualifications, each of them beaming with pride and passion as they shared their stories.

Why was this a problem?

Because I went straight from completing my high school certificate into a career as a manager at McDonald's, so no university for me. How was I going to match the impressive backgrounds of my colleagues on this training course? It got me thinking about my career at McDonald's and what it allowed me to achieve.

So, I lead off with my McDonald's story, culminating in the fact that I attended Hamburger University in Chicago Illinois, where I graduated with a Degree in Hamburgerology. Five years later, I was honoured to be a professor at Hamburger University based in Sydney, where I ran the international training course for the most senior managers and franchisees from the Asia Pacific region. This course was only offered in Chicago, London, and Sydney at the time.

So, here I was thinking I couldn't measure up to my fellow students at the coach training course, but to my surprise every one of them was in awe of my experience. For the next eight days, all they wanted to talk about was McDonald's.

I knew that Ray Kroc had a contemptuous opinion of MBAs and people who attended business school or obtained college degrees in management, believing they lacked competitive drive or market savvy. For a time, McDonald's had a policy of not hiring MBAs. He also forbade McDonald's executives to have secretaries and required them to answer their own phones. They were expected to follow dress and grooming rules similar to those of rank-and-file employees in the restaurants, which included no scruffy beards (though carefully groomed facial hair was allowed). And they received regular company pamphlets extolling thriftiness and financial responsibility both at the company and in their personal lives.

This thriftiness continued through my times at McDonald's and was best evidenced by all executives flying in economy regardless of status. I can remember sitting in economy next to our CEO on one trip overseas, when he could have easily been up the pointy end of the plane.

McDonald's is held in high regard, but I do believe standards have slipped in recent times. That could just be the self-righteous feelings of an old time McDonald's employee. It's funny how our memory recalls the fondest moments in our life. Back in the 1980s, 1990s, and 2000s, McDonald's was an employer of choice, and ex-McDonald's employees were given preferential treatment in the recruitment process by other employers, because of the recognition of the standards of excellence, discipline, and work ethic of a McDonald's employee.

Today, over 1.9 million people work at McDonald's, and in the USA, one in eight people have worked at McDonald's. My guess would be that more than 95% of those people would speak of their time in favourable terms. I would be surprised if there are many other businesses globally that could measure up to this.

It all started for me in the Strand McDonald's in Sydney's CBD, in March 1983, with my good mate Dave Benson. We did a couple of training shifts before our new store opened in April 1983 at Pitt & Park Street in the city.

The thing that struck me about the way McDonald's did business was the Assembly line process they employed, where everyone had one job to do. Everything was broken down into stations, which were separate areas where different components of the product assembly process took place. To make a burger, there was someone responsible for toasting buns, someone cooking each size of meat patty, someone designated to place all of the condiments on the toasted buns, someone to determine the production and wrap the burgers, someone to cook the fish, chicken, and apple pies, and someone to cook the French fries. And then in other parts of the store, there was someone to serve on register, to clean the dining room, and that was on a moderate shift. On busy shifts, we would have as many as 30-40 crew members on shift and a range of roles that you could not even imagine, like the gopher (who would have to *go for* this and *go for* that), the person who just made soft drinks, or someone just to sweep the floors.

The assembly line I referred to was actually created by the McDonald's brothers in 1948, and was termed the 'Speedie Service System'. This system delivered fresh, hot food orders and thick, cold milkshakes in an astonishingly short twenty seconds from the time a customer placed their order.

I remember my first shift at our new store. I was on dressing (putting the condiments on the toasted buns), and there was a precision to the way we did everything at McDonald's. I was dressing a run of Big Macs, and the procedure was to place two large size, or three regular size, pickles on the lettuce. They also needed to be spaced and not overlapping each other. It was busy, and one of my pickles had overlapped when an overzealous 18 year old manager named Sharon Atkinson observed my pickle situation as she walked past the dressing station. She quickly addressed the situation in a very assertive manner, and effectively said if I couldn't do it right, I shouldn't do it all—you decide!

For a split second, I did think about whether I wanted to continue or not. No one had ever questioned my competence or desire before, but I quickly realised this was good. I liked the discipline.

You'll be happy to know that Sharon and I are still great mates after more than 36 years. In fact, a few months into my McDonald's career, Sharon learnt that I was living on my own at 16 years of age in a studio apartment. She insisted that I move in with her. I didn't but I certainly appreciated her offer. That was how it was at McDonald's. We were like a family; everyone cared about each other and worked for, and looked out for, each other. Today, academics refer to this as Culture.

The discussion around vision, culture, and values are common place in business today, but back when McDonald's started in the 1950's it was not so common place. In fact, corporate culture was just starting to be discussed and used by managers, sociologists, and organisational theorists at the beginning of the 1980s.

The foundation of McDonald's success was created by Ray Kroc. Right from the first day he observed the McDonald's operation, he had a vision for the business and where it could go. He built on the foundations that were created by the McDonald's brothers, regarding the values and culture that they had established within the original McDonald's business.

I am going to talk more about culture and values in chapter 6, as this should be the foundation for any business .

Ray Kroc

There are a number of Kroc-isms and quotes from Ray Kroc throughout this book, because I have enormous respect for what he achieved. He left school as a 15 year old and went on to create an empire and the most recognised brand in the world.

Ray wasn't a fast food operator, but he created the world's most successful restaurant chain and pioneered modern day franchising, marketing, and philanthropy; or what we know nowadays as corporate social responsibility.

> *'You don't need to be a genius or a visionary, or even a college graduate for that matter, to be successful. You just need a framework and a Dream."*
>
> - **Michael Dell (Dell Computers)**

Ray Kroc believed that the success of his company lay in his franchisees following 'the McDonald's Method' to the letter. To ensure this, he developed a 75-page Operations manual that outlined every aspect of running a McDonald's business. Nothing was left to interpretation. Burgers had to be prepared exactly the same; served with a quarter ounce of onions, a teaspoon of mustard, and a tablespoon of ketchup. Fries had to be $\frac{1}{4}$ inch by $\frac{1}{4}$ inch thick and about 4-6 inches long. The manual even specified how often the restaurant needed to be cleaned.

In 1961, Kroc came up with a way to gain even greater control over his franchisees. In the basement of a McDonald's in Elk Grove, Illinois, he opened a training centre that would eventually become Hamburger University, where students earned their degrees in "Hamburgerology" with a minor in French fries. Since its establishment in 1961, over 80,000 students have graduated.

In 1983, McDonald's invested $40 million in Hamburger University, a 130,000-square foot facility on an 80 acre campus located at McDonald's Corporate Offices in Oak Brook, IL. This was an impressive campus with a 5-star Hyatt hotel on campus exclusively for McDonald's.

McDonald's has many recipes, but the overarching recipe that contributed to the businesses success was the principle of creating systems and then recruiting people to execute those systems.

McDonald's has a system and process for doing everything in the business. The obvious procedures relate to the production of the products and how they are delivered, but it went as far as obscure procedures like the flow rate and volume of water that came out of the faucets or the flush of the toilet, and the number of sesame seeds on a Big Mac bun.

The Process

Here's why McDonald's has been so successful.

They documented everything that needs to happen in the business, and any current day business owner should be able to do the same by completing the following steps.

Document

Document the steps that need to be performed in the business for every function. To do so, you need to ask yourself 6 key questions.

1. What is the procedure and why is it needed?
2. What is the outcome of doing this properly?
3. What is the process; the step-by-step procedure?
4. Who does the procedure?
5. What assistance, technology, equipment, or resources are needed?
6. How will you measure the success?

Once you have the procedure and have documented it, you have to train people how to complete the activity.

The owners responsibility is to create the system, and the people in the business are charged with the responsibility for actioning the system.

Train
Invest in training people using the systems and procedures that you have developed. Create a written procedure and then utilise technology, including video and digital platforms to deliver the 'how-to'.

Don't rely on the initial training you have provided. Regular evaluation and feedback reinforces the desired standards.

McDonald's were the first restaurant chain to receive college credits for their management development programs in the USA. Here in Australia, McDonald's was the first to receive the same recognition of prior learning (RPL) for its management development programs, earning credits towards a Masters of Business Administration (which is ironic considering Ray Kroc's views on MBAs). In 1995, McDonald's Australia achieved a Registered Training Organisation (RTO) status for the training it provides to all of its employees, and proudly offers industry recognised qualifications to all levels of employee.

Measure
McDonald's measures everything, and it started with Ray Kroc. It was not uncommon for Ray and his team to be standing in the store with a stop watch measuring the productivity, or assessing the quality of both raw and finished products. "You can't improve what you don't measure."

There was an acronym that became synonymous with McDonald's, and that was QSC&V. The core of the McDonald's principles of Quality, Service, Cleanliness, and Value (QSCV) lives on as the company's cornerstone to this day.

Every aspect of the store operation was assessed regularly, with a scored ranking and grading of each area of the restaurant. A store would be graded as A, B, C, or F. An acceptable score was a B grade, but everyone aspired for an A grade store, as this was key to the expandability of the McDonald's owner/operator.

Ray revolutionised franchising from the perspective that he did not grant large territories or regions with owners having multiple sites. He believed that the owner needed to operate a single site business to prove their ability to own and operate multiple locations. The measurement was a key component of the expandability criteria.

Be Daring, Be Different

By the 1950s, the concept of drive-in style service had become firmly established, and hamburgers and cars had become closely connected in the minds of many Americans. It was now possible for a customer to purchase a hamburger without getting out of a car, but the problem was it took up to 30 minutes to get your meal. Dick and Mac McDonald were pioneers, and were committed to making eating out more affordable and more desirable to the average American, so they introduced the 'Speedie Service System'.

'The Speedie Service System' replaced glassware and silverware with disposable items, and created a system in which each employee was only responsible for one step of food preparation. Carhops were eliminated, making customers responsible for retrieving their food. McDonald's boasted after putting in place 'the Speedie Service System', "Imagine—No Carhops—No Waitresses—No Dishwashers—No Bus Boys."

The new system allowed McDonald's to fire skilled short-ordered cooks, many of whom were enticed to taking higher paying jobs, and replace them with less skilled, minimum-wage workers. It increased efficiency, lowered prices, and increased the number of customers, having expanded to the working class.

McDonald's started as a hot dog business then became a hamburger business, and changed the way fast food restaurants operated. They became a business that grew through franchising and then through property ownership. McDonald's is the largest holder of real estate in the world.

Although it sounds like Ray Kroc had three businesses, hamburger restaurants, franchising and real estate, he focused on the core of the business: hamburgers, French fries, and drinks. He kept the menu simple and just made sure that they did it better than anyone else.

> **The main thing, is keeping the main thing, the main thing**
>
> **—German saying**

It is critical for a business owner to know what they are and what they want to be, then stick to it. It's easy for entrepreneurial business owners to get distracted by the new, shiny toy and feel like they have to take on every new product or idea in the market. But this can weaken your position and what you stand for, and runs the risk of confusing your customer about what you are.

I remember the mantra of Australia's first managing director and CEO, Peter Ritchie. He maintained Ray Kroc's approach to sticking to your core business, keeping your menu simple, and doing it better than everyone else. McDonald's USA had gone down a path of trying to be all things to all people, selling items like pizza, pasta, spaghetti, hot dogs, bread, and cookies in store, and some crazy seasonal products like lobster.

So be daring, be different, but don't be ridiculous. Know what you are, and just do it better than anyone else.

People

The biggest lesson I learnt from McDonald's was they weren't in the burger business; they were in the people business. Everything they did was about People.

They had processes for recruiting, onboarding, training, developing, and serving people. Never lose sight of the industry you're in. If people buy your widget, then you're in the people business.

McDonald's were phenomenal at recognising people, both their internal customers and their external customers.
As an internal customer, recognition of your performance happened on every shift. They were masters at giving feedback, both positive and corrective, and providing incentives and competitions to drive performance.

There were many programs for the crew: individual shift competitions for front and back area teams and individuals, monthly crew meetings with awards, team outings, inter-store competitions, crew member of the month, quarter, and year, incentive programs like McBucks where you would earn McDonald's money to redeem for prizes at a gala event. There were state and national competitions like SuperCrew or McOlympics where winners in each station (category) got the opportunity to represent their store, their state, and their country in an Olympic style competition, which saw participants actually getting to go the Olympics.

There were similar incentives for management, with outstanding performance awards where the recipient would receive McDonald's stock. There were annual awards and international conferences, and all the while there were impromptu awards and recognition given to top performers.

I learnt to look after people, have them share in the success of the business, because it is the people who deliver it.

<u>Takeaways</u>

❖ Create an assembly line of processes to streamline operations.

❖ Document your vision and values.

❖ Determine the culture you want in your business.

❖ Document every process and create procedures for every function.

❖ Create systems to measure performance.

❖ Focus on people.

❖ Have incentive programs and recognise performance.

CHAPTER 5

HAVE YOU GOT THE GUTS?

Leadership

"I never get the accountants in before I start up a business. It's done on gut feeling."

—Richard Branson

Leadership

In this chapter, I am going to discuss everything to do with guts and leadership, as I see it guts come into play in many ways as a business owner. Traditionally, when people refer to 'guts' in business they refer to the courage to make decisions. I want to extend on that and consider two other relevant references to 'guts'.

"All our dreams can come true if we have the courage to pursue them"
—Walt Disney

There are three inspirational stories of courage and persistence that I resonate with.

I love the story of Colonel Harland Sanders being rejected by 1,009 restaurants before one took on his recipe.

Walt Disney was turned down by 302 banks before getting the finance to fund Disneyland, and was fired from the Kansas City Star because the editor thought he "lacked imagination and had no good ideas."

Steve Jobs was sacked from Apple, the company he founded, but he came back and turned the business around.

The Two Other Guts You Need to Be Aware Of

1. Gut Feeling

Have you ever had a feeling in your gut, or felt that something just didn't feel quite right? This is referred to as intuition, a combination of our experiences, instinct, and senses.

Sometimes when you meet someone for the first time, you instinctively sense whether you can trust that person or not.

It has been said that women have better intuition than men, but all of us experience intuition or have those 'gut feelings'.

The reason I wanted to include this section, is that every time that I have felt something is not quite right or seems too good to be true, my intuition or 'gut feeling' has proven to be right. Sometimes, I have gone with my gut feeling, and other times I have not.

I believe the situation that you're in influences whether you make decisions rationally or emotionally. Don't get me wrong when I say emotionally, because that gives the impression that this may be a bad attribute. Sometimes your emotions just make sense and you should go with them.

I think I'm a good judge of character, but I am also characterised by extreme optimism. I tend to see the best in people and am quite trusting, but at times I haven't trusted myself and gone with my gut feeling. I've given people or situations the benefit of the doubt.

What I've recognised is, when I'm stressed or a little desperate, I can make bad decisions. When I'm under duress, I tend not to be as intuitive, and this is probably the time to be more rational.

I believe we need to trust our gut and use our intuition more, but we need to make sure we do it in times where we have a clear mind, free from stress. If you're under pressure, don't dismiss your intuition, but balance it with being more analytical.

Trust you gut instinct; it will usually be right.

2. Your Gut

Business owner health is of critical importance, but business owners work hard and often make the excuse that they don't have time to exercise, eat nutritious food, sleep long enough, and generally look after themselves. The reality is not that they don't have time—they just don't make time. They prioritise the business ahead of their personal health, but this has the effect of impacting our performance and can also make us a little resentful.

I'm overweight and guilty of all the excuses above, but I did something about it.

I was in a coaching session with one of my clients, Phil Raish. We were doing an update on his business since we were last together and discussing what his challenges were. He responded by saying everything is great. I didn't let him off the hook and, as we dug a little deeper, there was a problem.

Phil had been working ridiculous hours as his business was booming, but he had neglected his health. He wasn't exercising, was working long hours, was not getting enough sleep, and he was eating fast food and drinking alcohol. He said, "I'm the heaviest I've ever been," and he was 106kg. I responded by saying, "Me too, now let's do something about it." So, I set him a challenge, since both Phil and I are pretty competitive. Most business owners are.
Business owners like to win. They win new business, they win new contracts, they win awards, they win at life, and Phil is a

great example of this. Last year he bought another business and bolted it onto his existing business, and diversified into new sectors of his market. He was recognised in the NSW Business awards and won the Excellence in Customer Service Award and Outstanding Business Leader Award.

I set him an 10 week challenge to see who could lose the most weight. We had quite a bit of fun over those weeks giving each other a hard time, which made the chore of dieting and exercise more enjoyable. Plus, there was a prize on offer for the winner: $500 cash.

I told a number of people about the challenge, because when you do that, you have more accountability. Some of the people I told said I was crazy betting against Phil, because he's super competitive.

They were right! He smashed me and won the $500, and he lost over 20kg. I lost 8kg, which I was still happy with although I was $500 out of pocket. I lost some weight and continue to do so. I'm going to the gym, which makes feel so much better at work. I'm fitter, healthier, and more productive. The best part of it all, is that I have a client who is pretty happy with his achievement and how it has made him feel.

So, with the fact that business owners are winners, it's not surprising that they find it difficult to "lose" anything—including weight.

If you have a GUT, you need to do something about it. People who exercise, get enough quality sleep, and eat well also have better mental acuity, drive, focus, and performance, boosting efficiency on the job.

3. Guts in Business

If you're a business owner, you'll probably relate to this. You may have had feelings where you questioned why you ever got into business. You might have even contemplated how to get out. You might have had that sick feeling in the pit of your stomach to the point of actually being sick, worrying about the state of your business and the impact it had on the people around you and those that you love.

It was so much safer, and at times more enjoyable, being an employee with guaranteed salary, holiday and sick leave, bonuses, and incentives. Being able to clock off at the end of the day and not to have to worry about work until the next day, you were only responsible to yourself and the role you fulfilled. As a business owner, you're responsible for everyone and everything. There's no IT or marketing department to call on, no financial controller, and surplus funds in the bank account to meet payroll obligations or pay your suppliers when they're due.

You are no longer just responsible for your income. There's your family's welfare, your assets, and everything that you've worked so hard for. There's the employees who are part of your team, who you think of as your extended family. As a business owner, you have their livelihood and that of their families in your hands.

Why would anyone go into business? It takes guts, and it's all about risk. I believe there are 'risk-seekers' and 'risk-tolerators'. All business owners are risk takers, and while you have to be, the key is the calculated risk.

It might sound a little irresponsible to term a group of business owners as risk-seekers, because no one should actively seek risk. But there is an inevitability associated with business ownership that involves risk, and some business owners are more comfortable with risk.

Risk-seekers derive excitement from uncertainty. Have you ever driven your car around on empty when you could have just as easily filled up earlier? Do you ever schedule that extra meeting, when in reality there is no possible way you can fit it in? Heaven forbid you might have even run late for a flight or missed one completely, or dare I say it, been late for a meeting.

There's a pretty strong chance that if you're a risk-seeker, you like the adrenaline rush. You've probably driven too fast, bungee jumped, skydived, been around wild animals, or partaken in other adrenaline junkie type activity.

Risk-seekers are impatient and like doing multiple things, because we get a bit bored with too much detail, and we make decisions quickly. I'm only up to chapter 5, and I'm already thinking about when I can publish this book, and what the title and theme of my next book should be.

Risk-tolerators do not necessarily see it as risk. They pursue their goals by understanding, accepting, managing the inherent risks of the decisions that they make.

I have had partners in four of my businesses. I should probably start of by sharing with you that I am a risk-seeker, but I would only classify myself as mid-level and by no means extreme. I have a few of those kinds of business owners I coach and consult with, more about them a little later.

This may not be indicative of every business situation, but two of my business partners have been risk-tolerators, and coincidentally, they have both had excellent businesses that have been very financially rewarding. My other two business partners were probably more like me, and while the partnership was fun, it was nowhere near as profitable as it could have been.

The risk tolerant business owner spends more time analysing, understanding, and assessing the risks at hand, learning how best to mitigate them. These risk-tolerant individuals confront fear not with the risk-seeker's optimism, but with thoughtful analysis, management, and self-awareness techniques.

Where Do Guts come from?

The willingness to take risks is a combination of factors. I use DISC behavioural profiling quite a bit in my current business, and there are some common traits and profiles associated with the risk-seeking and risk-tolerant profiles. The factors that influence your preference are a result of your life and business experiences, which include the results you've encountered, when you've taken risk previously, and the support network you have around you.

External factors aside, some people are just more risk-hungry than others. While you cannot choose what degree of guts you're born with, it can help to know if you're naturally fearless, genetically risk-averse, or somewhere in between.

As an entrepreneur and business owner, you will likely have to deal with some failure. It may be small, like a bad product launch or the risk you took bringing in a key employee who didn't quite measure up, or it could in fact be business failure. I have two clients I'm working with right now, who have been into administration and bankruptcy in previous businesses. Coincidentally, both of them are risk-seekers, and are both characterised by strong resilience, an attribute that all business owners need. Both of these business owners have picked themselves up, dusted themselves off, and started another business venture, as it's in their DNA—it's who they are.

Henry Ford had two failed automobile businesses before finding success with the Ford motor company. R. H. Macy of department store chain Macy's had two failed retail businesses before the success of Macy's.

What Is Risk, Really?

Very often, the perceived risk of a situation outweighs the actual risk, leading to irrational behaviour. It's worth asking yourself what the worst thing that can happen is, and if a business failure is one of those things. For some people, it will be, as their whole being is wrapped up in the business they created. But for most people, you have the ability to start over either in business or employment. Just learn from your mistakes, and don't repeat them.

How to Be Gutsy

Guts give business builders the courage to make things happen, stick with it, and remain confident no matter the impediments you face.

Guts-driven entrepreneurs aren't fearless; they just know how to cope with, and maybe even thrive in, uncomfortable environments. They're the same people who crammed for their exams the night before, and often they thrived in high pressure situations.

Recognise that you already have guts, in that you're already in business or contemplating going into business; that takes guts.

The guts to endure lets us recognise that failure is not an option, but rather a reality. It's about remaining strong and resolute; persevere in the short-term to realise your longer-term goals. You will experience failure. Expect it, relish it, and learn from it.

And for those who are risk-seekers, try to take on characteristics of the risk tolerators, or consider getting one of them to join you in your business. Partnerships aren't easy, but they provide balance and discipline that often the risk-seeker lacks but so desperately needs.

"If you're not a risk taker, you should get the hell out of business."

"Take calculated risks. Act boldly and thoughtfully. Be an agile company."

—Ray Kroc

Guts Is Required in Leadership

Leadership requires courage and guts, but it's important to make the distinction between leadership and management, as they are typically not synonymous. You can lead without managing, and you can manage without leading, but the effective manager-leader uses both skills.

So, what's the difference?

Typically, managers manage things. Leaders lead people. When you are in control of an outcome like profitability or sales, good management is needed. Managers need to plan, measure, monitor, coordinate, solve, hire, fire, and do so many other things.

"Leadership is less about the position you hold than the influence you have, It's about doing world-class work, playing at your peak and leaving people better than you found them, it's about leading without a title."

—Robin Sharma, Author of The Monk Who Sold His Ferrari

Leadership should be thought of in four ways:

1. Owner of a business
    a. What are the essential skills of effective leaders?
    b. What are your responsibilities?
    c. Who should make decisions?
    d. What kind of leader you want to be?
2. Role Model—being the best you can be
3. Industry leadership—being the best in your category
4. Having the ability to influence an outcome

1. The Owner's Role in Leadership

Leadership does not come naturally to everyone, especially if a business owner was simply a good technician or someone with an idea and happened to start a business. Starting a business and getting it off the ground takes vision, resourcefulness, determination, and guts, but often the skill of leadership is missing.

In the context of a small business, leaders are required to create a sense of engagement with employees. Small teams need effective leaders. The leader should articulate their vision for the business, communicate it to the team and help everyone understand where they're going, and give everyone the tools and resources to get there.

There are 5 essential skills of effective leaders.

1. Vision, Strategy, and Planning
Once the vision and strategies required to achieve the vision are set, a plan needs to be created to ensure the specific details are completed to ensure success.

Teams perform best when they know the end goal and the steps needed to get there. It's essential for the owner to share the completion of tasks with the team in order to get things done. I don't believe employees should be involved in the setting of the vision of the business, as that is the vision of the business owner and what they want to achieve. Employees may influence the business owner's thoughts in this respect, but the vision in privately owned businesses should be the owners.

2. Collaboration
The team should be involved in the creation of the plan, as that will ensure a greater buy in and execution of assigned tasks.

One of the strengths of McDonald's was the single focus that individuals had in the business, within stores, with station and section responsibility, and then in middle management at Head office. Each division operated a little bit in isolation. Towards the end of my time with McDonald's, the business started involving all levels of middle management in the strategic planning process, which made us all feel like it was our strategic plan. I can still remember verbatim the positioning statement we created in 1996: "We'll give each customer, each and every customer, every time, an experience which sets new standards in value, service, quality, and cleanliness." While incorporating the famous QSC&V, it was done in a different order to focus on the value customers receive from their McDonald's experience.

Leaders who fail to encourage a spirit of collaboration have not created a company culture that values team achievements.

"None of us, is as good as all of us."

—Ray Kroc

Collaboration empowers employees with your confidence. It shows them that you trust them. It allows them to make contributions that go beyond their individual role, and makes them feel valued.

"Nobody cares how much you know until they know how much you care."

—Theodore Roosevelt

3. Decisiveness

As a business owner or leader, you're going to make mistakes. There's always going to be more information that could have helped you make a better decision.

Employees want and like to be led; that's often why they're employees. Decisiveness instils confidence as long as it is well thought out. It may be pertinent to share your thought process or rationale regarding your decisions, so your employees understand how you think and why you made a particular decision.

Good decisions make sense. If someone has to ask why you've made a decision, and you're frustrated by the fact that they don't understand, chances are your decision could use some improvement. Good decisions are easy to explain, and they're easy for your team to support.

Either way, a leader has to make decisions. Sometimes, those decisions are to allocate other people on your team to help out if they're qualified to do so.

This can be the hardest decision a business or leader ever has to make: the decision to let go and delegate to someone who may be able to do something better. But if you don't involve them in the process of decision making, then they will always revert to you, or worst still, they'll leave.

To assist with the decision making, it is worth understanding the process a leader should go through in determining the best course of action to take. Using the decision making model will assist with this.

The Decision Making Model

Observation and prioritisation form the basis for the decision-making model. This basic model should be used to balance the relationships with our team and customers, and the priorities of the business, in order to achieve our desired outcomes.

The purpose of the decision making model is to provide a structure for us to support and balance the operational needs of the business (PRIORITIES), with the needs and wants of our people (RELATIONSHIPS). At times, depending on the situation, it may be necessary to put more emphasis on one area than the other. The balance will tip in favour of that area. This is okay, provided you keep the other area in mind and work to restore the balance when possible.

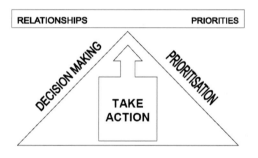

The observation component is the fact-gathering part of the decision making process. Once you have gathered your facts and organised your plan, it is time to MAKE A DECISION and TAKE ACTION. The word 'decision' is derived from a Latin word meaning 'to cut off from'. So, to *decide* is to *cut yourself off* from other possibilities. Once a firm decision is made, immediate action should follow. Never leave the place of a decision being made without taking some action step towards its completion.

4.Empathy

Empathy is the ability to understand and share in the feelings of another person. A leader must be able to understand how someone else is feeling. Leaders who embrace empathy understand that they must prioritize the needs of others.

Employees give a lot to businesses. In return, a good leader must truly care about their wellbeing.

Support

The previous four attributes form the foundation of the support that you should provide to your employees.

Support can come in many forms. It can be as simple taking an interest in them and what is important to them personally and professionally.

Support is about providing your team with a number of things, including access to you, access to the right resources so they can do their jobs well, knowledge that they are a key part of your team, and most importantly, that you are personally invested in the success of everyone who works for you.

Leadership Responsibilities

Leadership responsibilities are closely aligned to the five essential skills, but having the skills and using them are often things that leaders can lose sight of in the heat of the moment.

An effective leader needs to have a high level of emotional intelligence (often referred to as EQ), which enables them to make the right decisions for both the business and the people in the business.

Determine What Kind of Leader You Want to Be

Depending on what you read, you will see that there are anywhere between three and twelve leadership styles that can be used. For ease of reference, I am going to focus on the three most common leadership styles. Leadership styles are situational, and an effective leader needs to have the ability to move between the different styles depending on the situation. Most leaders do however have a predominant leadership style, just like they have a predominant DISC behavioural profile, and that is the style that they spend most time in and are most comfortable.

Having said that, as a leader with high emotional intelligence, you need to adjust your preferred style and make a conscious choice about the kind of leader that you want to be.

Autocratic or Authoritarian leadership   - Directive   -S1
Democratic or Participative leadership.   - Coaching   -S2
Paternalistic leadership   - Supportive   -S3
   - Delegating   - S4

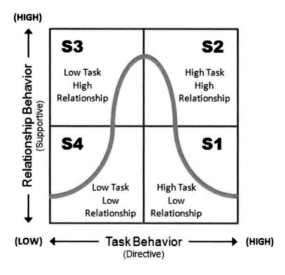

Let's use McDonald's as an example, and the leadership styles of the McDonald's brothers and Ray Kroc. Although they shared some common leadership traits, their approaches were significantly different, and that in part contributed to the ultimate falling out between the two parties.

The McDonald's brothers were S2/S3 style leaders: they were participative, paternalistic, and very focused on people. Ray Kroc was predominantly S1/S2: focused on the result and engaging people, and he took on a more democratic leadership style as the McDonald's business grew.

In the 2016 movie *The Founder*, Ray and the McDonald's brothers were portrayed as the opposite style leaders that they were.

Dick and Mac are portrayed as innovative men who care deeply about the quality of their product, their customers, and the people who work for them. They have an enormous pride in what they have created, which is very much an S2/S3 leadership style.

They inspired many future titans of the fast food industry, including Glen Bell, the founder of Taco Bell.

"There was a fraternity of us, and every one of us saw the McDonald's in San Bernardino and basically copied it after the boys gave us a tour"

—Glen Bell, Taco Bell

Jim Collins, head of Collins Food International remembered.

"We became good friends, and we all took our lessons from the McDonald brothers."

—Jim Collins, Collins Food International

Ray Kroc is portrayed as ruthless in the movie, and this was further exemplified by former Dire Strait's front man Mark Knopfler's solo song "Boom, Like That" in 2004.

Knopfler was amused by the fixations on the 'tall poppy syndrome' and people's fascination with success and apparent greed. Knopfler simply used phrases and comments that Ray actually said in his co-authored 1977 book, *Grinding It Out*, which detailed his often ruthless business practices. The book is referred to in the lyrics:

> *"But, man they made me grind it out, now"*

> **—Ray Kroc**

Several other Kroc quotes are paraphrased in the song lyrics, such as:

> *"If any of my competitors were drowning, I'd put a hose in their mouth and turn on the water." Which became "They're gonna drown; put a hose in their mouth."*

> **—Ray Kroc**

The phrase "Boom—like that!" is another Kroc-ism that gave the song its title.

> *"Look it is ridiculous to call this an industry. This is not. This is rat eat rat, dog eat dog. I'll kill 'em and I'm going to kill 'em before they kill me. You're talking about the American way of the survival of the fittest."*

> **—Ray Kroc**

The song is actually quite catchy. It's upbeat and infectious. If you haven't heard it, it's worth having a listen.

The Lyrics

I'm going to San Bernardino, ring-a-ding-ding
Milkshake mix is thus my thing now
These guys bought a heap in my stuff
And I gotta see a good thing shooting up now

Or my name is not Kroc, it's Kroc with a K
A crocodile is not spelt that way now
It's dog eat dog, rat eat rat
Kroc style, boom like that

Folks line up all down the street
Now I am seeing this girl devour her meat now
And then I get it, wham as clear as day
My pulse begins to hammer then I hear a voice say

These boys have got this down
Ought to be one of these in every town
These boys have got the touch
It's clean as a whistle and it don't cost much

You might be wondering why I have included this negative portrayal of Ray Kroc, but it's out there in the public forum, and unfortunately modern day media and the quest for entertainment has the tendency to portray people a certain way in order to sell more product.

That said, Ray Kroc was driven, and sometimes this can be perceived as aggressive. Sometimes, you need to be, particularly in the early days of establishing a business. Think about this in the context of how you want to be remembered and what your leadership style and subsequent legacy will be.

The business owner and often founder has had to do an amazing job to establish and grow a business. Often, the founder is a visionary and great at getting an idea off the ground, but there are some attributes the founder needs to be aware of.

1. Know your strengths and weaknesses. Focus on your strengths and recruit to support your weaknesses.
2. Focus primarily on what you're passionate about.
3. Don't accept excuses or see obstacles and challenges as impediments to your success.
4. If you want something, ask. The worst people can do is say no. I find business owners like sharing their experiences with other business owners. The Alternative Board (my business) has made a global business out of this.
5. Know when you need help, and ask for it or seek it out.
6. Know your limitations as a CEO. If you're not the right person to take the business to the next level, accept it and do something about it.

I was at a peer advisory board meeting in December 2018. There was a very successful business founder and owner at the meeting, and her topic for discussion was the appointment of a CEO. She stated there is no one else in Australia with the technical knowledge or connections in her highly specialised field. She acknowledged that she didn't feel like she was the right person to scale the business and take it to the next level. She wanted to appoint a CEO, but she was only looking to pay a salary of around $120k and didn't want this person making decisions about the business. She just wanted them to execute her plans and get approval for all decisions. Her peer board gave her a range of suggestions. Her take away was she didn't need a CEO, and that she probably only needed a General Manager who could progress once they demonstrated their ability, and she had the trust to delegate the decision making responsibility. As a founder, you need to determine when to bring in the right people to help your business grow to the next level, and you need to understand what you actually want them to do.

There is one critical factor to consider when you do appoint someone, which is best illustrated in the story "The Monkey Trap".

There are many variations to this story. In South America, Africa. and Asia, the natives have devised a very effective method of trapping monkeys. The plan is deceptively simple: the natives take a gourd or some similar object and drill a hole just large enough for a monkey's hand to pass through. They add some extra weight to the gourd with sand or pebbles, then put a nut or some fruit inside and place the gourd where a monkey will find it.

Here's what happens: the monkey sticks his hand through the hole to get the food—but with the prize in its grasp, the monkey cannot get its hand back out. The hole is too small for the monkey's hand to pass through, so long as it's holding the treat, and the gourd is too heavy for the creature to carry. Because the monkey won't let go of its prize, it's trapped, and the natives capture the monkey.

The lesson here is, sometimes we have to let go of things in order to get what we want. So, as a business owner or founder, it's knowing when to let go of responsibility or authority for the decision making, and when you need to bring the right people into the business.

Takeaways

❖ Go with your gut feeling.

❖ Focus on your personal health.

❖ Make calculated and well thought out risks.

❖ Leaders determine every aspect of what is acceptable in the business.

❖ Determine the kind of leader you want to be.

❖ Adjust your leadership style to suit the person and circumstance.

❖ Know when to let go and when to bring more senior people into your business.

CHAPTER 6

WHERE'S THE VALUE?

A Values Driven Business

"Price is what you pay. Value is what you get".

—Warren Buffett

A VALUES DRIVEN BUSINESS

There is a difference between value and values; both are important in business, but we should always start with our values in order to create value.

Initially, a business's values are aligned to those of the owner and founder, but evolve over time based on experiences. The business owner's values are the things that they believe are important in the way they live and work.

They should determine your priorities, and deep down, they're probably the measures you use to tell if your life is turning out the way you want it to.

As a business owner, you need to determine what is important to you, how you want to live your life, and how, or if, you can incorporate your values into your business. I found that my values were influenced by my experiences, both good and bad. I've tried to replicate the values I appreciated in others while attempting to not be like those I disliked.

In the acknowledgements section of this book, I started by saying that.

"I believe at the core of every person are their values and what they stand for, and these are shaped by the people we encounter throughout our lives, but in particular in the early stages of our development."

—Doug Downer

Once you have identified your values, they need to be distilled down to a group of core values. There will initially be a large number of values that may be important to you, but your core values should be the few things that make you unique. That's why I recommend no more than 3-4 core values. The other values may be secondary, or categorised as a set of traits.

Core values are the fundamental beliefs of a person or organisation. These guiding principles dictate behaviour and can help people understand the difference between right and wrong. Core values also help companies to determine if they are on the right path, and fulfilling their goals, by creating a guideline of how to act and behave.

Too many companies identify a large number of values, and like company mission and vision statements, no one in the business remembers them all. Therefore, they cannot live them. Keep it simple and meaningful—what makes you unique?

Core values can't just be a series of words. Each of the values needs to have meaning and context. I have listed a number of international companies, most of which have presence here in Australia, that have been acknowledged for living their core values. All have four core values, and all have a description of what they mean:

H&M

"Individually our values may seem obvious. But put them together and our unique company culture is born. Our values are part of who we are, what we stand for and how we act."

- **We Are One Team**—Our great colleagues make the difference. It's when we share our skills, knowledge and experience we become one team. Diversity makes us strong.
- **Entrepreneurial Spirit**—The day we stop acting like entrepreneurs, we'll be just another fashion company.
- **Straightforward and Open-Minded**—We value diversity in people and ideas, as much as in personal style.
- **Cost-Conscious**—Being cost-conscious is about keeping an eye on expenses and making smart, sustainable choices even in the small, everyday things.

Southwest Airlines

"Above all, Employees will be provided the same concern, respect, and caring attitude within the organisation that they are expected to share externally with every Southwest Customer."

- **Warrior Spirit**—Strive to be the best. Display a sense of urgency. Never give up.
- **Servant's Heart**—Follow The Golden Rule. Treat others with respect. Embrace our Southwest Family.
- **Fun-LUVing Attitude**—Be a passionate Team Player. Don't take yourself too seriously. Celebrate successes
- **Wow Our Customers**—Deliver world-class Hospitality. Create memorable connections. Be famous for friendly service.

Deloitte

"Our shared values are timeless. They succinctly describe the core principles that distinguish the Deloitte culture."

- **Integrity**—We believe that nothing is more important than our reputation, and behaving with the highest levels of integrity is fundamental to who we are.

- **Commitment to Each Other**—We believe that our culture of borderless collegiality is a competitive advantage for us, and we go to great lengths to nurture it and preserve it.
- **Strength From Cultural Diversity**—We believe that working with people of different backgrounds, cultures, and thinking styles helps our people grow into better professionals and leaders.
- **Outstanding Values to Markets & Clients**—We play a critical role in helping both the capital markets and our member firm clients operate more effectively. We consider this role a privilege, and we know it requires constant vigilance and unrelenting commitment.

KPMG

"Our Values create a sense of shared identity within the KPMG organisation, which is a network of member firms in 152 countries. They define what we stand for and how we do things."

- **We Lead by Example**—At all levels we act in a way that exemplifies what we expect of each other and our member firms' clients.
- **We Respect the Individual**—We respect people for who they are and for their knowledge, skills and experience as individuals and team members.
- **We Are Committed to Our Communities**—We act as responsible corporate citizens by broadening our skills, experience and perspectives through work in our communities and protecting the environment.
- **We Are Open And Honest in Our Communication**—We share information, insight and advice frequently and constructively and manage tough situations with courage and candour.

Airbnb

"No global movement springs from individuals. It takes an entire team united behind something big. Together, we work hard, we laugh a lot, we brainstorm nonstop, we use hundreds of Post-Its a week, and we give the best high-fives in town."

- **Be a Host**—Care for others and make them feel like they belong. Encourage others to participate to their fullest/ Listen, communicate openly and set clear expectations.
- **Champion the Mission**—Prioritise work that advances the mission and positively impacts the community. Build with the long-term in mind. Actively participate in the community and culture.
- **Be a Serial Entrepreneur**—Be bold and apply original thinking. Imagine the ideal outcome. Be resourceful to make the outcome a reality
- **Embrace the Adventure**—Be curious, ask for help, and demonstrate an ability to grow. Own and learn from mistakes. Bring joy and optimism to work.

IKEA

"We believe that every individual has something valuable to offer and we strive to have the same values in the way we work."

- **Leadership By Example**—Our managers try to set a good example, and expect the same of IKEA co-workers.
- **Daring to Be Different**—We question old solutions and, if we have a better idea, we are willing to change.
- **Togetherness and Enthusiasm**—Together, we have the power to solve seemingly unsolvable problems. We do it all the time.
- **Accept and Delegate Responsibility**—We promote co-workers with potential and stimulate them to surpass their expectations. Sure, people make mistakes. But they learn from them!

The Alternative Board
I thought I would share with you the core values of my business, The Alternative Board in Australia. The acronym I have used is GAME and reflects the four core values.

Growth
Personal, Professional & Business growth.

Authenticity
Develop deep relationships through honesty and being yourself.

More
Work with business owners that want More—More time, money, balance, sales, profit, whatever their More is.

Excellence
Ensure Excellence in everything what we do and be recognised as a market leader.

I believe that business is like a game; there's a set of rules, competitiveness, results, and it should be fun.

While in the USA in 2018, I wanted to go Chick-Fil-A, which is a chicken restaurant. I had heard such positive stories about this business and their products. The business was founded in May 1946. It operates more than 2,200 restaurants, primarily in the United States.

Many of the company's values are influenced by the religious beliefs of its late founder, S. Truett Cathy, a devout Southern Baptist. Most notably, all Chick-fil-A restaurants are closed for business on Sundays, Thanksgiving, and Christmas.

Their Mission is:

To glorify God by being a faithful steward of all that is entrusted to us and to have a positive influence on all who come into contact with Chick-fil-A.

Core Values
- Customer First
- Personal Excellence
- Continuous Improvement
- Working Together
- Stewardship

The average store turnover is 4 times the volume of a KFC in the USA, and they only open 6 days a week. On a per store basis extrapolated over a full week, they would rank as the number one quick service restaurant, ahead of McDonald's. If they were to open on Sundays, they would take another $1 billion in yearly sales.

The business is driven by its Christian values and the desire to give its staff time off from work to attend worship if they so choose. For them, values are more important than money, and they are widely respected by customers and the broader marketplace.

Corporate social responsibility (CSR) and philanthropy have become synonymous with businesses in recent times, and form part of the values of many organisations.

Auntie Anne's pretzels in the USA was founded by Anne F. Beiler and her husband. From day one 30 years ago, giving back has been woven into the fabric of the company. "Auntie" Anne Beiler started baking pretzels to help fund her husband's desire to provide free family counselling services for their community. He ultimately realised his dream and opened a counselling centre.

"Caring for other people is the purpose of Auntie Anne's."

- **Anne F. Beiler**

Anne started her business as a market stall with the sole purpose of their philanthropic desires.

Closer to home, there are two Australian companies that I had a little to do with, and both businesses have philanthropy at the core of their business. Sam Price is the founder of Mexican chain Zambrero, Coco Mexico, Mejico, Kid Kyoto, and Indu restaurant brands. Zambrero has given away nearly 28 million meals in its Plate for Plate charity, and Sam Prince has also created a charity called One Disease. I know from recruiting team members for Sam that and employee's values and what they stand for is key to joining his team.

I was watching the Ethnic Business Awards in December 2018. I love to see inspirational stories of new Australians making good, and the appreciation they have for the opportunities that coming to Australia has given them. I was chuffed to see Alf and Nadia Taylor win the award for best medium to large business in Australia. Alf and Nadia are the owners of TNA Solutions, and through the success of that business they have created The Nadia and Alf Taylor Foundation, which has supported over 150 charities across 39 countries, and has directly impacted the lives of over 19,000 people, while donating millions of dollars to charitable organisations.

McDonald's established Ronald McDonald House Charities and Ronald McDonald Houses to give back to the community, which is one of their core values. I believe any business that operates in a community, needs to be an active part of that community. It's not just good business, but it's a good value. It's becoming more of a differentiator with the new generation of workers coming through, particularly with Millennials who want to be part of, and use products from, businesses that are charitable and responsible.

I've mentioned previously that most businesses are in the business of people, and that an important part of any company's values should be giving back to the community that supports them—it's just good business.

Value Proposition

Once you have established your core values, which are your guiding principles internally, you need to turn your attention to what that means to the customers you are going to deal with.

A value proposition refers to a business or marketing statement that a company uses, to summarise why a consumer should buy a product or use a service. This statement convinces a potential consumer that one particular product or service will add more value, or better solve a problem, than other similar offerings will. Companies use this statement to target customers who will benefit most from using the company's products.

The value proposition has to be quantifiable, and needs to talk to the measurable benefits that your product or service delivers. Too often, companies don't articulate the measurability attached to the value they bring. If you can do that, a customer will have a better idea of exactly what you can do to help solve their problem, rather than just a creative combination of words.

I have two businesses, firstly as the Franchisor for The Alternative Board in Australia. We are in the business of providing strategic advice, coaching, and consulting for small to medium size businesses. There are a number of ways I add value to these businesses. Once I uncover what their true pain points are, I am able to articulate my value proposition to suit their requirements.

I also have a franchise consulting business called Franchise Ready, which works with business owners who want to scale and grow their business through a franchise model.

At The Alternative Board, in my capacity as a business coach, the most measurable value that I deliver to my clients is increasing their revenue. I currently work with over 40 businesses, and the average sales growth of my clients in 2018 was in excess of 50%.

In my other business, Franchise Ready, I have helped launch 15 emerging franchisors by establishing their strategy and action plan for expansion and franchising. These emerging franchisor businesses have grown on average by over 200% in the first year of working with me.

So, I want to share with you how to create your own value proposition using my two businesses as examples.

To do this, you need to answer a number of questions. We use a proprietary strategic planning tool called business builder's blueprint in The Alternative Board business, and here are the questions we ask when helping a business owner articulate their value proposition.

1. What is the specific Value you provide?

2. How are you differentiated from your competitors?

3. Describe your ideal customer.

4. What is the problem that you solve?

5. What is the customer's need or current dissatisfaction?

6. How is that unlike your competitors?

7. Your product or service is?

The Alternative Board—Example

What is the specific value you provide?
Access to the collective wisdom of successful business owners, who simulate your own board of directors and assist you with the decision making in your business. Strategic planning and advice to help businesses grow.

How are you differentiated from your competitors?
No lock in contracts with a money-back guarantee. All of our coaches are business owners just like you and we are based in your local area.

Describe your ideal customer.
A Business owner who wants more; more sales, more time, more profit, more control over their business and personal life.

What is the problem that you solve?
Helping business owners make better decisions, and providing them with a sounding board and a trusted business advisor.

What is the customer's need or current dissatisfaction?
Not being locked in to an expensive coaching program with no guarantee of results.

How is that unlike your competitors?
We offer a month-to-month membership proposition, so we don't lock people into long-term agreements. They stay as long as they are getting value and stay with us on average over 4 years.

What is your product or service is?
Business owner peer advisory board meetings, strategic business coaching, and business planning tools.

"We help business owners have better businesses and better lives by helping them to make better decisions through Business Owner Advisory Boards and Strategic One on One coaching sessions that in 2018 resulted in sales growth in excess of 50%."

Franchise Ready —Example

What is the specific value you provide?

Helping growing business grow quicker and more efficiently through the creation of strategy, documentation, implementation, and support. The businesses that I helped launch in 2018 have grown by over 200%.

How are you differentiated from your competitors?

Have operated at every level within franchise and non-franchise businesses. Not just a consultant, I see myself as part of the team for the businesses that I work with. I don't just want one-off consulting work; I want a long term relationship.

Describe your ideal customer.

A proven and successful business that has the capacity to scale but just doesn't know how to.

What is the problem you solve?

Create the strategic plan and all the requisite documentation required to start franchising. I make franchising your business easier and quicker.

What is the customers need or current dissatisfaction?

Value for money and a comprehensive solution.

How is that unlike your competitors?

Pricing is more competitive and materials are superior.

Your product or service is?

The development of a comprehensive strategic plan that enables businesses to scale and grow through franchising, and includes the execution of all documentation and ongoing support.

"In 2018, We helped 15 Good Businesses become Great Businesses by helping them grow through Franchising. We offer a comprehensive solution that includes creation, development, implementation and ongoing support which in 2018 resulted in business growth in excess of 200%".

Takeaways

❖ Create a values-driven business.

❖ Focus on 3-4 Core values.

❖ Value = <u>Experience</u>
             Price

❖ Consider a corporate social responsibility (CSR) program.

❖ Create a powerful and measurable value proposition. It needs to quantify the value you bring and the problem you solve.

CHAPTER 7

HOW WE DO THINGS AROUND HERE

The Business Model and Systems

"Build systems within each business function, let Systems run the business and people run the systems. People come and go but the systems remain constant."

—Michael Gerber

The Business Model and Systems

What came first, the chicken or the egg? Some may argue that a business needs to articulate the business model first, and then create the systems and processes to drive the business model.

I believe that every business is born out of the embryo of an idea that gets fleshed out and built into a business. Although there will be an initial business model around how the business may work, that is all theoretical. It is not until you create and perfect the processes that you know where to take the business model.

The McDonald's brothers are a really good example of this. Their original business was a hot dog business, but it had some challenges associated with the speed of service, the labour component, and the type of crowd that was attracted to the 'carhop waitresses'. After a couple years in business, the brothers began making plans to renovate their business model based on the lessons they had learned, and the hamburger model of the McDonald's business was born.

In my current business, The Alternative Board, we surveyed hundreds of business owners and asked them what their key learnings were from opening their businesses, and what they would have done differently if they had their time over. Only 18% of them wished they had started with a better business model. So, as long as you start with a business model, it can evolve over time.

In this chapter, we will discuss processes required in creating systems, processes, and a business model that works.

It seems obvious that having a system should make things easier, but I think a lot of people believe it's difficult. Perhaps this is because they don't have experience creating systems, and as humans we typically don't like change. Learning and implementing something new requires change.

In order for a business to work, it has to be modelled on an existing system or process that has been proven to work.

Systems are not designed to complicate business, but to simplify.

There are systems in every aspect of our life. It's what give us order and keeps things under control. If you think about our life, systems start in families with the way we are expected to behave. When we are old enough, we go to school and progress through the school system, and school is designed to prepare us for future life. It requires discipline; to get up in the morning, pack lunch, catch the bus on time, move between classes, learn, study, and hopefully graduate.

There are systems in all relationships, whether they be interpersonal, friendships, or lovers. In all relationships, there are expected behaviours. In business, there are methods and processes that cause us to act in a certain way. Every country has a political system, whether you like them or not, and there is a way that we as a population are governed. So, as you can see, systems are in action in every aspect of our lives.

In chapter one, The Foundations of Growth, we discussed the stages of business growth, and how having systems and processes helps you move through the various stages more quickly. The longer you wait to systemise your operation, the longer it may take to move through the stages of business growth.

The reality is, if something needs to be completed in a business, there needs to be a procedure for it. It doesn't need to be perfect to start with, as it will get perfected over time.

I remember when I left McDonald's, I had just spent the last three years in the training department creating, updating, and maintaining all of the training materials. To date, it is still the most systemised business that I have ever seen.

When I left McDonald's, I joined a retail food business called the Foodco Group, who had two brands: Muffin Break and Jamaica Blue. This business had just over 100 stores, and I was staggered by this. This was not because it wasn't a good business, but because their operations manual was a lever arch folder that consisted of some very basic procedures and a series of memos. And there were no real documented systems or processes, and certainly nowhere near as sophisticated as where I had come from at McDonald's.

I remember James Fitzgerald, the owner of Foodco and the man who hired me, was concerned about me coming from such a structured background; whether I would handle the lesser structure of the Foodco business. He said to me, people who come out of McDonald's never make it in their next role, because it's such a culture shock to them.

Don't get me wrong, business doesn't have to be that systemised either, but if you're going to complete a function in business there's a process. It just needs to be documented and the best person to do that is the person who performs the function. Someone who's good at writing can pretty it up later.

"Done is Better than Perfect"

—Mark Zuckerberg

At Foodco, we recruited the perfect person to pull this project together. Her name was Natalie Brennan, and that was back in 2001. Nat is still there, and she is now running the Muffin Break business, and the Foodco Group has grown significantly with over 600 stores operating in 7 countries. There are a lot of contributing factors to this growth, but in my mind perfecting the system contributed significantly to this achievement.

I think back to my time at McDonald's starting in 1983 and just over 100 stores. Today, they have close to 1,000 in Australia, and I can tell you that systems and processes have evolved significantly. I say this because every business gets better over time. Ray Kroc's first operations manual was 75 pages. When I left in 1997, one of the ten operations manual chapters was that big.

So, What Is a Business Model?

At its core, your business model is a description of how your business makes money. It's an explanation of how you deliver value to your customers at an appropriate cost.

In their simplest forms, business models can be broken into three parts:

1. **Cost of Goods**: Everything it takes to make something: design, raw materials, manufacturing, labour, and so on.
2. **Cost of Sales**: Everything it takes to sell that product: marketing, distribution, delivering a service, and processing the sale.
3. **Pricing & Payment**: How and what the customer pays: pricing strategy, payment methods, payment timing, and so on.

Franchise Business Model

In a franchise business model, you are allowing the franchisee the blueprint for starting and running a proven business model to someone else. You're providing access to a national brand and support services that help the new franchise owner get up and running. In effect, you're granting access to a successful business model that you've developed.

Understanding the problem you are solving for your customers is undoubtedly the biggest challenge you'll face when you're starting a business. Customers need to want what you are selling, and your product needs to solve a real problem.

But ensuring that your product fits the needs of the market is only one part of starting a successful business.

The other key ingredient is figuring out how you're going to make money. This is where your business model comes into play.

There are a number of questions that you need to ask yourself and evaluate.

1. What is the problem that your business or product solves?
2. Is there a market for your goods and services?
3. Who are the competitors in your market?
4. What are their strengths and weaknesses?
5. Does your product or sector have a life cycle, and what stage is it up to?

A business model needs to include a description of a company's:

- Products
- Target customers
- Value proposition
- Distribution channels
- Core capabilities
- Commercial network
- Partnership model
- Cost structure
- Revenue model

The Business Model Canvas

The Business Model Canvas was proposed by Alexander Osterwalder based on his early book: *Business Model Ontology*. It outlines nine segments, which form the building blocks for the business model in a nice one-page canvas. You can find a detailed explanation in his bestselling book, *Business Model Generation*.

The Business Model Canvas reflects systematically on your business model, so you can focus on the creation of your business model segment by segment.

This also means you can start by brainstorming and filling out the segments that spring to your mind first, and then work on the empty segments to close the gaps. The following list with questions will help you brainstorm and compare several variations and ideas for your next business model innovation.

For each of the nine sections of the business model canvas, there are a number of questions to assists you in completing each segment of the canvas. These are just examples to get your juices flowing.

For those of you that have a well-established business, you might be thinking, "I already have a business model in place." That may well be the case, but every business needs to evolve their business model, so this exercise and the questions are worth visiting each year as part of your strategic planning activities.

You may recall in chapter one, I introduced the idea of the internal franchisee and the external franchisee. So, if you're thinking of scaling the business, changing the business model, and potentially involving other stakeholders in the business, then this process is essential.

The Business Model Canvas

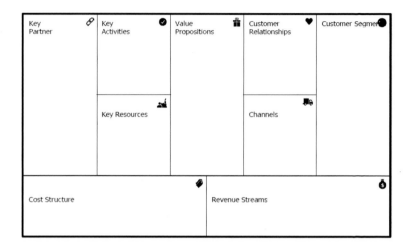

Key Partners
1. Who are your key partners/suppliers?
2. What are the motivations for the partnerships?

Key Activities
1. What key activities does your value proposition require?
2. What activities are the most important in distribution channels, customer relationships, and revenue stream?

Value Proposition
1. What core value do you deliver to the customer?
2. Which customer needs are you satisfying?

Customer Relationships
1. What relationship does the target customer expects you to establish?
2. How can you integrate that into your business in terms of cost and format?

Customer Segment
1. Which classes are you creating values for?
2. Who is your most important customer?

Key Resource
1. What key resources does your value proposition require?
2. What resources are the most important in distribution channels, customer relationships, and revenue streams?

Distribution Channel
1. Through which channels do your customers want to be reached?
2. Which channels work best? How much do they cost? How can they be integrated into your and your customers' routines?

Cost Structure
1. What are the biggest costs in your business?
2. Which key resources/activities are most expensive?

Revenue Stream
1. What are your customers willing to pay?
2. What and how do they pay recently? How would they prefer to pay?
3. How much does every revenue stream contribute to the overall revenues?

Once you have completed your plans for the business model, you need to know what options are available to you, the business owner, as your way to move forward.

As an example, let's take a look at Airbnb's business model using the business model canvas.

Airbnb

Airbnb is an online marketplace that enables people to list, find, and rent accommodations (single rooms, apartments, houses) for a processing fee.

Unique Selling Proposition (USP)

The biggest accommodation provider in the world does not own a single room. Airbnb does not rent the accommodation from the host but conveys only between supply and demand. Their business model builds on the share economy and on the strong belief that home owners are willing to rent out free space to strangers.

The Business Model Canvas

airbnb

Key Partners

- Investors (Greylock Partners, Sequoia Capital, Y Combinator)
- Online payment providers (PayPal, Western Union)
- Local photographers
- Traveler networks

Key Activities

- Online platform development & maintenance
- Community management
- Marketing
- Videos & Photography

Key Resources

- Platform
- Listings
- Brand
- Community of travellers & hosts

Value Propositions

- Trusted community marketplace for people to list, discover and book unique accommodations around the world
- Monetize unused resources

Customer Relationships

- Fast, reliable and secure customer service
- High performing website, App, Local brand ambassadors
- 24/7 support

Channels

- Website, App, Blog, Facebook, Youtube, Twitter
- Paid advertising
- Referral (via friends)

Customer Segments

Guests:
- Budget travelers
- Business travelers
- Travelers who want a difference experience

Hosts:
- Residential owners who have extra place to rent

Cost Structure

- Platform development and maintenance costs
- Marketing and community management costs
- Business development costs
- Insurances
- Online payments

Revenue Streams

- 6-12% of booking fee for guests
- 3% of booking fee for hosts

In chapter six, I introduced you to a business called Chick-fil-A. I wanted to share their business model with you. Other than being driven by their values, their business model is quite unique. Chick-fil-A retains ownership of each restaurant.

Chick-fil-A selects the restaurant location and builds it, and they have a unique franchise model where a franchisee only needs to pay a $10,000 initial investment to become an operator. Each operator is handpicked and goes through a rigorous training program; the interviews plus training can take months, and it's not an easy process. Chick-fil-A states on their franchising website:

"This is not the right opportunity for you if you:
- Are seeking a passive investment in a business.
- Want to sell property to Chick-fil-A, Inc.
- Are requesting that Chick-fil-A, Inc. build at a specified location.
- Are seeking multi-unit franchise opportunities."

They are in huge demand because the business model works, and they are super selective when choosing their business partners. For a $10,000 initial investment, the franchisee typically earns around $100,000. This is double the average wage earner and double the profit of the average small business owner in the USA.

They are selective in who they allow to join the business from team members through to franchisees. It's not uncommon to have more than ten interviews, and they often tell applicants, *"If you don't intend to be here for life, you needn't apply."*

And with less than 5% operator turnover and team member turnover 50% less than other fast food restaurants, their model is working.

Intellectual Property

So, once you have established your business model, you need to document it and protect it.

Intellectual property (IP) represents the property or creations of your mind or intellect. If you develop a new product, service, process, or idea, it belongs to you and is considered your IP.

Entrepreneurs and business owners need to understand the basics of intellectual property (IP) law to best protect hard-earned creations and ideas from unfair competition. Intellectual property includes distinctive items that someone has created, and those that give the owner an economic benefit.

Trade Secrets

A trade secret is a formula, process, device, or other business information that companies keep private to give a business advantage over competitors. Intellectual property examples of common trade secrets include, manufacturing processes, client lists, ingredients, systems, sales methods, launch strategies, and your business plan.

Unlike the other types of intellectual property, a business can't obtain protection by registering the trade secret. Protection lasts only as long as the business takes the necessary steps to control disclosure and use of the information.

One of the most famous examples of trade secrets is the original formula for Coca Cola. The company claims that it is only ever known to two people at a time, and they are not allowed to travel together. If one dies, the survivor is required to choose a successor and reveal the secret to that person.

Tips for Protecting Your IP

An owner may seek professional experience from an intellectual property lawyer to help the company plan for success and avoid theft of ideas, designs, and other concepts.

1. Include IP considerations when developing your business plan.

2. Consider trademarks. A trademark and a business name are two different things. Registering a business name doesn't give you exclusive rights over that name.

3. Take responsibility: It is up to you to manage and renew your IP registration.

4. Avoid publicising your idea. You may not be able to get a patent if you have discussed, demonstrated, or sold your creation. If you need to discuss your idea with other people, make sure they sign a confidentiality agreement.

5. IP is for everyone. IP protection is available to anyone, regardless of business size.

Types of IP protection

There are seven types of IP protection, but most businesses use these four—patents, trademarks, designs, and copyright.

Patents: A patent is a right granted for any device, substance, method, or process which is new, innovative, and useful. A patent gives the owner the exclusive right to the invention for a period of time and can be legally enforced.

I have a client who bought a national business from the original owner when his patent expired after 20 years. The prior owner couldn't see the value in the business once his patent expired, but the business had so many other elements that only needed to be adjusted. My client introduced some new complimentary products and services, and has started franchising the business and significantly reinvented the business model.

Trademarks

A trademark is used to distinguish the goods and services of one business from those of another.

A trademark can be a letter, number, word, phrase, sound, smell, shape, logo, picture and/or an aspect of packaging.

It is not compulsory to register a trademark, but it is important to consider if you want to retain exclusive rights to its use. Some of the best examples of brands that have been trademarked are Nike (with its Swoosh), McDonald's (with its Arches and the business name), Apple (with its Apple logo, fonts, and colours), and for obvious reasons it can't trademark the word apple, but interestingly, they have a legal department that will send you letters if they feel you are impinging on their trademark. We had one of our clients sent a letter to this effect.

Registering a business, company, or domain name is not the same as trademarking it, and may not provide you with exclusive rights or ownership of the name.

Designs

A design refers to the features of shape, configuration, pattern, or ornamentation which give a product a unique appearance, and must be new and distinctive in order to be registered. A registered design allows the owner to use it for commercial purposes, to licence, or sell it.

Registered designs tend to relate to form, while patents relate to function. A fashion designer can register a design IP relating to the function and appearance of the garment, while the creation of a material that is unique would be more of a patent.

Copyright

Copyright is a free and automatic legal right given to the authors or creators of original works. You can copyright works but not ideas.

Copyright is commonly applied to music, sound recordings, art, books, films, and on and off-line publications.
Computer programs and databases may also be copyright protected.

Summary

Registering a business, company, or domain name does not give you exclusive rights like a registered IP does. If you register a business, company, or domain name, you do not automatically have the right to use that name as a trade mark.

If you plans to scale and grow your business, or you just don't want somebody else to copy you, it is wise to register your IP and protect the hard work you have put into establishing it.

Let's Identify Your IP

In understanding what your IP is, we need to differentiate between the products, intellectual property, and the output. Look at the examples in the table below and complete the same exercise for your business.

Brand	Product	Intellectual Property	Output
McDonald's	Hamburgers	Franchising	Royalties
McDonald's	Restaurants	Property owned & leased	Rental margin
Airbnb	Property rentals	Sharing platform	Commission
Apple	Technology	Innovation	Advocates
Your Business			

The Key Benefits of Systems

Systems set the *expectations* for the team and the customers, and ensure *consistency* in all aspects of the business. It enables you to have better *operations*, which engages your teams because they know how to do their jobs effectively. This *saves money* by increasing *productivity* and positively impacts the *profitability* of the business. This ultimately enables *scalability* of a business, which is what every business wants regardless of whether they want to franchise or not.

What are some of the systems you need to create?

Once you have developed your business model, you need to create the systems that will enable you to execute on the business model. There are a number of systems that need to be created, such as:

- Standard Operating Procedures (SOP's)
- Operations Manual
- Training Manual
- Measurement processes
- Administration
- Finance
- Human Resources
- Product Supply

Standard Operating Procedures (SOPs)

The starting point for developing systems within a business is creating a set of standard operating procedures. These should start with the day-to-day operations of a business that involve creating the products and selling them to your customer. The process that is used can be carried across every other system you develop within the business.

Let me share with you a McDonald's example of a Standard Operating Procedure: how they used to serve a customer.

It was referred to as the 'Six Steps of Service'. Some of these steps will resonate with you if you've ever been a customer at McDonald's, and you may have even been annoyed by the 'Six Steps'.

The Six Steps were:

1. **Smile and greet the customer.**
    a. You were even given examples of what to say like, "Hi, How are you?" or "Good afternoon, may I take your order?" We were even encouraged to get to know regulars by name and use their name in the greeting.
    b. We all had to wear name badges so customers knew who we were.
    c. Later on, they developed a service culture called 'hand in the air service' where crew members would raise their arms to let the customer know they were ready to serve them. We always wanted to be waiting on customers and not have them waiting on us.

2. **Take the order and suggestive sell.**
   a. Let the customer decide on their menu items of choice and enter the products onto the computerised cash register system.
   b. The computerised cash register system broke the menu down into main menu categories: main meal, sides, beverages and desserts.
   c. The register would prompt the crew member if a menu item from one of the four categories wasn't chosen.
   d. The crew member would suggestive-sell an item; you may have heard, "Would you like fries with that"?

That one question has enabled them to serve more than 30 million serves of French fries per day.

I think where we may have annoyed people is when we then tried to suggestive sell a large size, or then offered for a beverage or dessert. McDonald's had a system to train 15 year old kids how to sell and make millions of dollars. The system worked!

   e. Determine if the order is to eat in or take away.
   f. For dine in orders, place the serving tray on the counter with the tray liner facing the customer.
   g. Total the order and enter as dine in or take away.
   h. Inform the customer of the total amount of the order.

3. **Assemble the Order.**
   a. There was a process to the order in which you retrieved the menu items, drinks first, main menu items, fries, and then desserts. This process ensured the product was presented in its optimum condition (hot or cold as need be).

4. Present the order
Dine in orders

a. There was a designated position to place each item; the drinks were the heaviest and most prone to fall off the tray, so they were placed on the right hand side of the customers tray, as right handed people make up 90% of the population, so the right hand is the strongest for carrying weight.

b. The burger went on the left hand side, and the fries were to be stood upright against the burger to ensure they presented well.

c. The desserts were placed next to the cold beverages.

Take away orders

a. Open the appropriate size bag (size 4, 8, 12) depending on the number and size of the menu items. Each menu item had a number assigned to it to determine what could fit in each sized bag.

b. Place the burger in first, then fries on the side or top of the burger, and then hot desert items.

c. Double fold the bag towards the crew member. Present the bag with the logo facing the customer.

d. Place the beverage on the customers right hand side of the bag.

e. If there are more than 2 cold items (beverages and desserts), then place them in a 2 or 4 cup tray.

5. **Receive payment**
   a. Restate the amount of the order to the customer.
   b. Receive the money from the customer and state the amount received ("That's $8 from $10").
   c. Lay the notes across the cash draw in case a customer says they have given you a different denomination.
   d. Count the change back to customer.
   e. Place the notes in the draw in the correct section with the heads of the notes facing in the same direction.
6. **Thank customer and ask for repeat business**
   a. Thank the customer by saying something like, "Thank you, please call again," or, "Please enjoy your meal, see you next time."

I know I went in to quite a bit of detail with this example, but that was to illustrate the point, that to be successful a business needs to think about every permutation in the process of developing a standard procedure.

To continue with the example of McDonald's Customer service procedure, it is important to document the steps prescriptively. But you need to be careful that it is still sincere and authentic.

I remember my first trip to the Gold Coast in Queensland in 1985, and I went to McDonald's on Cavill Avenue. I got served by a surfer dude with long curly blond hair and a great tan, and he spoke like a surfer dude.

He used the McDonald's 'Six Steps of Service', but he was authentic to who he was. When asking me if I was dining in or taking away, he said, "Is that to munch in or munch out?" I thought this was brilliant, because it was exactly who he was.

From that moment on, I tried to do exactly the same.

So, have a documented procedure but enable your team to put their own personality into the delivery of that procedure.

In creating a set of standard operating procedures, they need to be documented into a checklist of steps to be completed. In order to create the checklist, you need to answer these six key questions:

1. What is the procedure and why is it needed?
2. What is the outcome of doing this properly?
3. What is the process—the step-by-step procedure?
4. Who does the procedure?
5. What assistance is needed? Technology, equipment, resources?
6. How will you measure the success?

Operations manual

Once the standard operating procedures have been created, they need to be placed into a manual that outlines all of the businesses operations It's like an encyclopedia of all the company know-how, and gives your team members the processes and procedures for running the business. It covers all of the intellectual property of the business, and it sets out what operational excellence looks like, and outlines the key performance parameters.

Most operations manuals set out the standards, how to complete them, and how to remedy problems should they occur. It's like a troubleshooting guide for the business that can be used as the reference guide for the people in the business when a problem or challenge occurs.

The primary reason for an operations manual is to house the standards and intellectual property of the business, and to be used to train employees by establishing the minimum standards. Operations manuals need to be documented, and most progressive businesses have moved these resources to an online portal. This way, they can be changed easily and regularly and, and they can be accessible for all employees.

Operations manuals should include some core information that is usually divided into sections or chapters, depending on the size and complexity of the business.

Sections of operations manuals

Every Operations manual should have some standard sections, such as:

1. Introduction
   - Organisational Chart
   - Job descriptions
   - Contact details
   - Company History
   - Company Values
2. Products and Services
   - Includes all the product specifications
   - How to make and sell the products
3. Documented processes and systems.
   - All of the standard operating procedures
4. Equipment
   - How to use and maintain equipment
5. Occupational Health and Safety
   - Risk management
   - Emergency procedures
6. Human Resources
   - How to recruit, induct, train, and performance manage the team
7. Policies and Procedures
   - Staff policies—expected behaviours
8. Business Administration
   - All office administration
   - Finance function
9. Management and Leadership
   - Used to develop the leadership team

Training Manual

The training manual should be a building block program that provides structure to the development of people within the business. It should start with the basics of the business and builds, and becomes more detailed as the employee is developed through the business. The manual starts with the introduction and induction of the personnel, and move into the standard operating procedures before progressing into management and leadership.

Measurement Processes

The Operations manual details the standards, but there needs to be a system and process for measuring performance. There needs to be established standards or criteria and a scored assessment that measures the standards. There's a great saying, *"You can't manage what you can't measure,"* by legendary management consultant Peter Drucker, which basically means that you can't know whether or not you are successful unless success is defined and tracked.

Administration

The way the business is administered needs to be documented and include all agreements, contracts and office procedures. The best people to do this are the people that complete the tasks every day.

Finance

The business needs to determine the company set up and how the finance function will be administered, including the accounting software, chart of accounts, and how to manage the cash flow and financial reporting.

Human Resources

The business needs a system for how they determine the recruitment needs, how to recruit, onboard, train, performance manage, and provide succession opportunities. I have stated this earlier: every business that sells a product or service is actually in the people business, so you need to have a system for managing the human resource function.

Product

There are three components to the product.

1. Cost of goods: everything it takes to make something, which includes design, raw materials, manufacturing, labour, and so on. You need a system for determining what products you need and how you are going to negotiate the appropriate purchase price.

2. Cost of sales: everything it takes to sell that product: marketing, distribution, delivering a service, and processing the sale. It is important to develop the optimum cost of creating the product or service for sale.

3. Pricing and payment: how and what the customer pays and includes the pricing strategy, payment methods, payment timing, and so on. This requires the business owner to determine where they want to position their product in the market (low, mid, high), and what methods of payment they will accept to assist with cashflow.

Every aspect of a business needs to be documented, and a system for completing all aspects of the business is required.

So, get started and document every aspect of what you and your team do, so that it can be turned into a procedure and form part of your system.

"You must perfect every fundamental of your business if you expect it to perform well"

—Ray Kroc

<u>Takeaways</u>

❖ Start documenting your procedures as soon as possible. It doesn't have to be perfect to start with.

❖ Create your business model using the lean canvas model.

❖ Register your IP, trademarks, trade secrets, and copyright.

❖ Create a system for each function within the business.

❖ Document the systems into an operations manual.

CHAPTER 8

THE MOST IMPORTANT INGREDIENT

People

"Clients do not come first. Employees come first. If you take care of your employees, they will take care of the clients."

—Richard Branson

PEOPLE

I don't care what you make or do; if you sell it and you have customers, then it involves people, and that means you're in the people business. Understanding people is essential in business. There are way smarter and more relevant commentators on psychology and people related matters than me, but I want to share with you my experience, as it related to people in a business and how important people are to your success.

In chapter 8, I referred to a quote by Michael Gerber:

> *"Build systems within each business function, let systems run the business and people run the systems. People come and go but the systems remain constant."*

Systems are the foundation of building a replicable business process and ensuring a consistent approach to the delivery of the ideal outcome, but people make it happen.

So, I think a good starting point is understanding yourself and why you are different. The reality is that we are all different, but we also have remarkable similarities. People can be categorised into two main groups in business as I see it:

1. Entrepreneurs/business owners/self-employed
2. Employees

Almost everyone started as an employee and for some reason they decided to take a different path. There are many things to like about employment, and for everyone there are things we dislike. But when the dislike becomes too much, we create change. We either confront the issue and resolve it, or we move on, to another employment opportunity, or for many with an entrepreneurial spirit, their own venture.

To properly understand people we need to understand ourselves, and then some basic principles relating to the core needs that people have; whether you subscribe to Maslow's hierarchy of human needs or Antony Robbins definition of the 6 core needs. It is worth understanding at a base level what drives or motivates human behaviour.

A great mate of mine and former business partner, Jim Davidson, is a master practitioner in the area of organisational development and the use of behavioural profiling, and he uses the 6 core needs in his training and facilitation.

Here is a basic summary of the 6 core needs

1. Certainty
2. Variety
3. Significance
4. Connection
5. Growth
6. Contribution

At a fundamental level, people's behaviour is driven to allow them to meet these 6 core needs. Typically, people have two dominant needs, but all are required to some degree.

The need for certainty, variety, significance, and connection are for the most part performance related, while growth and contribution are related to personal satisfaction

The typical behavioural characteristics of each core need is:

1. **Certainty:** order, control, security, avoidance of pain, and safety.
2. **Variety:** adventure, novelty, pleasure, freedom, the unknown, change, and newness.
3. **Significance:** individuality, importance, and feeling unique, special, or needed.
4. **Connection:** communication, approval, and attachment.
5. **Growth:** learning, personal development, an expansion of capacity, and capability.
6. **Contribution:** service, care, giving, and support.

I am a big fan of using psychometric profiling to better understand people. There are a number of products in the market, and how deep you would like to go will determine which profiling tool that you will use. I like, and have used, the DISC model extensively over my career, as it goes deep but not so deep that it becomes too complicated; let's leave that for the psychologists.

There is a direct correlation between the 6 Core needs and DISC:

D Style: Wants—Certainty and Significance
I Style: Wants—Variety and Connection
S Style: Wants—Certainty and Connection
C Style: Wants—Certainty and Significance

- Procrastination is a negative behaviour that fulfils certainty.
- Boredom can be too much certainty.
- The need for certainty can hold you back.
- Systemisation is a way of providing certainty within your business.

With people at the core of every business and decision that is made, it is critical that the owner or leader of a business has high emotional intelligence and self-awareness. This is so they can lead and manage themselves and the people in their business.

The starting point for any business should be for the owner of the business to articulate the kind of business they want to have, and this starts by establishing the values of the business.

Chapter two introduced the importance of values in an organisation. They are the guiding principles that should dictate the expected behaviours and can help people understand the difference between right and wrong. When bringing people into a business, it is important that the prospective employees values are in alignment with the values of the owner and the business.

"Culture eats strategy for breakfast."

—Peter Drucker

A business owner needs to create the strategy for their business, and part of that strategy is to define the values and the desired behaviours or culture of the business. The creation of the ideals for the desired culture need to be at the foundation of the strategic plan, and should form one of the critical success factors or goals of the business. This goal area needs to be well thought out, and incorporate all of the elements of a strong people plan, which we will cover in this chapter.

Only then can 'culture eat strategy for breakfast', because the culture of the people in the business and their actions will be the ones to execute the business strategy.

The values influence the company culture of a business. The concept of company culture was first raised in the 1950s and became more readily discussed in the late 1980s and early 1990s. It had been a very difficult thing to describe until recent times, as it was more of a feeling of the team in a business. This is partly because culture is best described as the unspoken behaviours, mindsets, and social interactions within a business.

We didn't know that it was called culture back in 1983 when I started working at McDonald's, but when I look back now, what we did, how we did it, and why we did it, was all related to the culture that was created in that business.

Culture is the reason people join, stay, or leave an organisation. There's a famous saying that 'people don't leave jobs, they leave managers'. I believe there to be an element of truth in that statement, but how is the manager allowed to create a reason for an employee to leave an organisation? I believe it's because an element of the culture of that business is not right. A culture that allows an employee to decide to leave because of an individual is not supporting the team aspect of culture, because culture should be the way everyone behaves in an organisation.

People are drawn to organisations that have characteristics and values similar to their own; organisations are more likely to select individuals who seem to 'fit in', and over time those who don't fit in tend to leave.

Culture is omnipresent and needs to evolve over time, but should always be aligned to the company's values and form part of the strategic plan. Just because it exists, does not mean it doesn't need attention. It should be part of the annual planning process each year, with activities scheduled to ensure the culture evolves and stays strong.

Some Great Examples of Culture Done Right

I worked at McDonald's for fourteen years. I started at 16 and I worked 3-5 times a week while at high school. I would volunteer for double shifts, work till 2am and back up at 6am the next day. There were occasions when I would 'close' the store and then perform the overnight 'maintenance' cleaning of the store, which resulted in working up to a 16 hour shift. I never said no when the manager's rang me up to come into work, and when I was there, I worked hard (sweated pickle buckets was the phrase).

When I started, I was getting paid $2.82, an hour and my first pay check was for just over $8,. I made more money collecting 'money bottles' when I was 8 years old, so it certainly wasn't for the money. As a manager I would work 60 hours a week without questioning it. I did what I did as a crew member and as a manager, because I loved it.

The reason was twofold: firstly culture and secondly systems. Interestingly, the culture was part of the system, what made it work so well. No one told you that you had to work excessive hours, but there was an expectation that you worked hard. We were always busy, and we were very profitable, because we had good systems and highly engaged team members where everyone was results oriented.

Culture is a feeling and an expected behaviour and it's self-governing by the people you work with. At McDonald's. it was all about the people. My best and longest standing friends are from my time at McDonald's. You either loved or hated your time at McDonald's. If you were there for more than six months, you know the culture and you enjoyed it. It was often referred to as having ketchup or Mac sauce in your veins. I know that all the ex-McDonald's people reading this will be smiling and nodding their heads in agreement.

When I left McDonald's I started working at Foodco, the franchisor for Muffin Break and Jamaica Blue cafés. I left with a strong understanding of systems and the importance of culture, and I implemented what I had learnt into that business.

In my eight years with the Foodco business, a significant number of key people I worked with at McDonald's joined me at Foodco. They then went into some subsequent businesses that I did, and I put this down to the fact that those people enjoyed the culture and leadership that I provided. A number of my friends and colleagues from McDonald's who left and went to other businesses, also had many of their team members join them in new businesses too.

This may sound contradictory to my earlier statement about the strength of the McDonald's culture, but I believe it speaks more to what we learnt at McDonald's about culture and how important it is and how to create it in other organisations. I have many friends who are still at McDonald's after 30-40 years. Many of them are now owner-operators (franchisees), which reinforces the strength of the culture. I know that these colleagues are still perpetuating the culture that existed back in the early 80's when we worked together.

The reason for mentioning the Foodco business, other than those McDonald's team members who joined me, is to illustrate the power of a strong culture. I employed many people at Foodco, and a significant proportion of them (more than 10) are still there after 20 years, in an age where the average tenure in roles is less than 5 years. Many of the others who may have left are either in senior management roles creating their own cultures, or have started their own businesses and created great culture in them. They experienced a strong culture in their time at Foodco, and they knew the power of a strong culture and how to get it.

The Foundations of Effective People practices

I learnt the foundation of how to manage the most important ingredient in business—which is people—in my time at McDonald's, and then further developed this in other roles. McDonald's was strong and had great systems, but we were siloed. Part of their success was, it was like a production line, and everyone had a defined role and you specialised in a particular role. We also had HR, or what was called an employee relations teams, to help with the administration of people practices. This positioned McDonald's as an employer of first choice.

All of this was great while you were there, but when I left and what I subsequently learnt, is that there aren't many other businesses that operate like McDonald's. In smaller businesses, you have to deal with things yourself, and at Foodco I actually became the pseudo HR manager with no qualifications. I put into place the principles that I learnt at McDonald's, and I have developed these throughout my career. But from a practical standpoint, as I said earlier, the only qualification I have is my Bachelor of Hamburgerology, I believe that if you treat people well and respectfully, and then couple this with process, you can't go wrong.

So, I want to discuss the processes that you need to operate within your business, to ensure the people side enables you to deliver the results that you are looking to achieve.

There are six steps to getting the people puzzle right:
1. Recruitment
2. Induction
3. Training
4. Performance management
5. Retention and Motivation
6. Succession

Recruitment

It all starts with a quality recruitment process. It doesn't matter how good your business, systems, or training are; if the raw ingredients (people) are rotten, the recipe won't work.

"People are our most important ingredient"

—Ray Kroc

Before you start the recruitment process, there are some basic activities to complete that will assist you with your recruitment.

- Create an organisational chart that outlines current roles and requirements, and also future requirements and likely timelines for the appointment of new roles.
- Create job descriptions for each role and ensure that they have the values and expected behaviours included.
- Create a budget to determine the calibre of new employee, and research the market to ascertain the market value of the best people in that role.
- Advertise the opportunity internally, if appropriate, but ensure all existing employees go through the same rigor as external applicants.
- Complete the pre-recruitment checklist so that you ensure that the business is well positioned to attract the best talent.

Job Descriptions

The main purpose of any job description is to outline the main duties and responsibilities that are involved in a particular job. Job descriptions are a communication tool that enable both employees and prospective employees to clearly understand the expectations of the role, its essential duties, the competencies and responsibilities, and the required educational credentials and experience.

Many business owners might have never written a job description previously, so they often avoid it. But there is a simple process you can use to document what you need from your team in each role.

Below are the questions that should be asked to create a job description:

1. What actual duties will the employee perform?
2. What are the time requirements for the job?
3. What minimum experience should the employee have?
4. What minimum aptitude should the employee possess?
5. What type of personality/behaviours should the employee have?
6. What is the corporate culture under which the employee must operate?
7. What type of training will be required?
8. Are there physical qualifications needed for the job?
9. How does the job help lead the corporate vision?
10. What are the performance standards?
11. How will performance be measured?
12. What are the soft skills required to do the job?
13. What are the hard skills required to do the job?

Once you know what you need, you can start recruiting for it.

The Recruitment Cycle

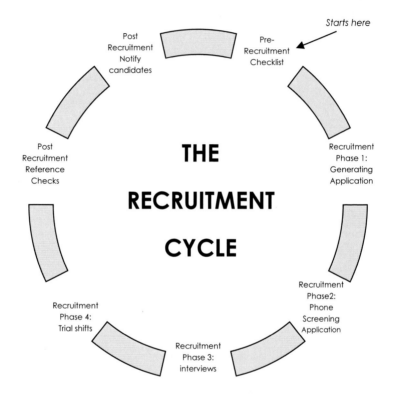

It is very important that the business establish a process for conducting their recruitment endeavours, and that they consistently follow that process to ensure consistency in the recruitment of the team.

The starting point for recruitment should be the completion of the pre-recruitment checklist.

Pre-Recruitment Checklist

Check Point	✓	Comments/Rationale	✓
Appearance Are the businesses' location and team members appearance presentable and appealing?		Prospective employees like to imagine themselves working in a fun, dynamic environment that they can be proud of.	
Customer Experience How are the Customer Experience levels when dealing with your business?		Prospective employees want to work in a place they would likely buy from or visit.	
Team Morale How do your existing Team feel about working in your business? Is morale generally high or low?		Prospective employees will either ask existing team directly or observe for signs of good or poor morale. Teams will be more likely to recommend you as an employer if they truly enjoy their own jobs.	
Training Is there a Training System being fully utilized in your business? Is the Training System working well?		Team will be more likely to recommend the business as a great place to work if they feel that they are being challenged and are receiving training.	
Recruitment Administration Do you have established Job Descriptions? Have you scheduled time for the Interviews?		Documented expectations for the prospective employee is critical, so you can match their skills and experience to your requirements. It is critical that you plan to spend enough time conducting the interviews.	

Ownership Thinking

There is a significant difference between an employee mindset and an ownership mindset ,and there is nothing wrong with either, It's a personal choice, and quite frankly, as a business owner we need employees, as they are the lifeblood of our business. The best business has employees who help the owner achieve their goals, by taking on responsibilities that the owner can't, or doesn't want to, do.

Business owners make things happen, they take risks, and they think long term, hence the need to be strategic. If you're a business owner, your business typically won't yield a consistent level of income for a number of years. But when it does, it will be significantly higher than the majority of employees (with the exception of highly paid senior executives in blue chip firms). In fact, more than 65% of millionaires are business owners.

Employees typically think short term, many are risk adverse, and they yearn for security. They wait to be paid, whereas the business owners gets paid when they want, and the employee waits for direction and to be told what to do.

The goal of any business owner should be to encourage an ownership mindset among their employees, so that the employees work together with the business owner to achieve goals more quickly.

An ownership mindset is where an individual or team takes accountability for the quality and success of both the output and outcomes of their work. Both of these are important, as ownership doesn't mean perfection. It means knowing why you are doing the work (the outcome) and making sure that what you produce (the output) is at the required standard. It means understanding, learning, and challenging, rather than following instructions.

The best way to develop an ownership mindset is for the owner to have an ownership mindset themselves, and then to mentor key people within the business. Employees like to mimic their boss, so the standards and mindset of the boss will rub off on the employees.

Identifying the right people in your business who have a business owner mindset or propensity for one is important. All business owners need to delegate and empower their teams to get things done, so finding the right people who you can nurture and develop will make your life and business much better. The key to this is having a structured succession plan and incentive programs in place, to encourage and motivate employees to aspire for more. In every business, there are those who achieve and there are those who don't. So, not everyone in your business needs to be promoted. But they will feel more important and give greater output if they get to act and are treated like business owners.

I saved the most important component of recruitment for last, as it is actually the last step in the recruitment process, and absolutely the most important part: reference checking. I have seen too often people making hiring decisions based purely on resumes and interviews without checking with past employers. This is critical and best explained in the saying 'past performance predicts future performance'. Do not hire anyone without conducting at least two reference checks with employers listed on the employees resume.

One could write a book on the six steps of the people puzzle, and I have mentioned the most important aspect, which is recruitment. If you don't get the right people, you won't get the right outcome even if the other five elements are strong. There's an old saying: 'hire for attitude and train for skills'. You can teach skills, but if the person doesn't fit your culture and have the right attitude, it's very hard to change them. So, let's briefly focus on the other five elements that you need to follow once you recruit the right people:

- Induction
- Training
- Performance management
- Retention and Motivation
- Succession

Induction

You may have heard the saying 'first impressions are lasting impressions'. Hence, the correct induction of new members to your business is important. Induction is the process of introducing a new employee to the company culture and the processes you use. The goal is to bring them up to speed as quickly as possible, as well as making them feel socially comfortable and aware of the expectations and their responsibilities.

It's important to have a process documented and well prepared for every employee who joins your business. It demonstrates your commitment to them, and if done correctly, makes them feel at ease. Most new employees experience both excitement and trepidation when starting a new role, and a good induction process can capitalise on the excitement and put them at ease.

When inductions are not done, or are done badly, the right exchange of information is not received by the new hire. This can result in their inability to fulfil the expectations of the role. Preparation and documentation of what has been covered ensures that every new employee is given the best opportunity to be successful.

Training

Even the best athletes need to train to perform at their optimum level; this is just as critical within an organisation. The role of training is to provide the skills and knowledge an employee needs to do their job effectively. Having a system to ensure the consistency of the delivery of the training, which will ultimately result in the consistency of execution of the job and operations, is the by-product of an effective training program.

I love the one where the CFO says to the CEO, "What happens if we train them and they leave"? and the CEO says, "What happens if we don't and they stay"?

Training is in fact an investment on the part of the business, the trainer and the trainee. The business invests time and resources (in the form of money) to develop the skills of the trainee, so that they develop their value and worth to the company by becoming a more competent and confident employee. The trainer invests their own time, energy, and effort to meet the businesses outcomes and provide the highest level of learning for the trainee. finally, the trainee invests their time, energy, and effort to develop themselves as a more effective employee for the business, improve their own work satisfaction, and/or advance through promotion.

The benefits to the business of an effective training program is increased productivity, greater employee retention, and greater business success.

The development of a training program using the systems, policies and procedures that have been developed is imperative to ensure consistency in the training of new and existing employees and consistency in operational standards and the training program needs to be documented, implemented and verified to ensure it's being used effectively.

Performance Management

Performance management isn't just about giving someone a performance review, that's important. But it's about having a system for measuring the performance of the business, a business unit or department, and the individuals in a business.

Having a method for measuring performance of every activity is important in business. Remember? 'You can't improve what you don't measure.' You will recall earlier in this chapter I described how to create a job description. That section refers to the questions that need to be answered to determine the role or in chapter 4. I discussed the questions you need to answer to build your processes. Both of those sections will assist you to determine what needs to be measured and how to measure what success looks like.

Performance management from a team member perspective can be as simple as knowing your team and taking a genuine interest in them. Talk to them every day, know what's important to them, and look for opportunities to catch them doing something right. All too often, we focus on catching people doing it wrong, but this slight shift in focus will have a dramatic impact on your culture. Informal feedback is important, but equally important is a formal review. This should be documented and provides the opportunity for the employee to be part of the review by giving feedback and agreeing on what needs to change. These reviews should happen at least every six months and potentially be linked to performance based wage reviews.

I used to own a business with Jim Davidson called Performance Culture, which Jim now runs on his own, and the whole purpose of that business was to assist business owners and CEO's create a high performance culture. This was done through the provision of training for managers and team members, on how to perform at a higher level through effective communication and reviews of performance.

Performance management can be very detailed, but it should also be very simple, and it's a matter of effective and regular communication between people in a business.

Retention and Motivation

The goal of all of these people principles is to have motivated staff that stays with you for as long as you want them in your business. If employees are happy and motivated, this should result in better business performance.

If team members are motivated and enjoy what they do, they will stay as long as the business can meet their objectives and give them what they want and need. So, it's important that the leaders of organisations understand the key drivers and motivators of their employees. This can be identified through the simple act of asking them, and performance reviews are often the best time to do this. If you choose to use behavioural profiling tools like DISC, they can provide you with these indicators that will assist you to motivate your people and help them achieve their goals.

I have all too often seen leaders trying to motivate people using the techniques or incentives that motivate themselves. It's important to know that everybody is motivated by different things, so it's important to know what motivates your team.

In my business with The Alternative Board, we always get our members (business owners) to articulate their personal vision. This is what they want their business to deliver to them personally. Business leaders and owners should do the same thing with their employees. When you know what they want, you can work towards helping your people achieve what's important to them.

I have a belief that motivation is an internal decision or motive, to behave in a certain way to achieve something that the person really wants. I am often torn when I hear people listen to motivational speakers or rely on people to motivate them. I don't believe that a leader (or motivational speakers) can motivate people to do something. I believe a leader has the responsibility to create the environment where expected behaviours are met. Leaders can inspire people to take action, but motivation comes from the individual. If they are not motivated to do something, often they won't. If it relates to work, the role of the leader is to ensure the team member performs at the agreeable standard, and to provide enough incentive that the employee is motivated to perform. This is where it is important to understand the key drivers or motivators of people on your team.

Don't get me wrong, I love incentives and programs that inspire me to perform better and to get recognition. As a High 'D' with DISC behavioural profiling, I love recognition, so incentive programs motivate me. But here's the thing: each behavioural profile has different motivational factors or drivers, and you need to know what motivates your team and the individuals on those teams.

Succession
Over 90% of McDonald's Managers started as crew members and were provided the opportunity to progress through the ranks much like myself. McDonald's have very clear development and training programs that provide a road map for employees to progress through the business. If you can keep the right people in your business for extended periods of time, the benefits to the business are enormous in terms of productivity, retention, and the direct effect of profitability. Every business needs to develop a program that shows people in the business how they can develop and progress.

How the People Equation Relates to the Business Owner

There's two sides to this People equation: the majority of this chapter has been dedicated to the people practices that a leader needs to employ in dealing with people within their business. This next section deals with the business owner, and will help you understand the profiles of a business owner, If you're considering becoming a business owner, here's what you need to be aware of in selecting the type of business you go into. For those of you who are considering franchising your business, you will need to think of this in the context of the type of people you bring into your franchise system as franchisees.

Three Types of Business Owners

While there is no single behavioural style or motivator that makes a successful business owner, there are similarities shared by the most successful. John Warrillow, best-selling author of *Built to Sell*, and creator of The Value Builder System, has developed three contrasting profiles that provide a simple model for classifying the three most common business owner types.

1. **The Craftsman**: a highly skilled person who creates a business because they know how to create a superior product. The custom motorcycle builder, the donut maker, the smart-phone app developer. Their energy is primarily focused on the creation of the product that they provide and less on running and growing a business. Michael Gerber refers to these types of business owners as technicians in his book *The E-Myth*.

2. **The Mountain Climber**: sees the development of their business as a series of hurdles to cross and a series of peaks to ascend. While they possess a strong drive to succeed, they never find true satisfaction in their work. Each conquered goal is followed by an even loftier one. Once they have created a successful company, they are not content to just run it. Instead, they conquered that

challenge— now, on to the next one.

I have to admit to being guilty of this. I have always owned a business while employed on a fulltime basis, and since leaving paid employment, I have had as few as three businesses at any given time. I like building things.

The beauty of my current business, The Alternative Board, is that it has enabled me to harness my need to build businesses by working with other business owners and effectively becoming part of their team. I have personally coached over 100 businesses in the past four years as their trusted advisor and business coach, and have been able to get intimately involved in the development of more than 15 new franchise brands in the past 18 months. This enables me to quench my first for building successful businesses and moving on to the next project.

I want to comment on the new generation of business owner that I have encountered in the past three years. There is a huge increase in the amount of millennial business owners, of over 40 business owners I coach at the moment, more than 20 of them are late 20s and early 30s. The reason I mention this, is that nearly all of them are 'mountain climbers'. This next generation of business owner are very different to the older and more experienced business owners I work with, who tend to be more like 'craftsman' and tend to have had their businesses for much longer periods of time (Over 15 years). This is compared to the millennial business owners I work with, who want to build, flip, and be out within five years so they can move onto the next project.

3. **The Freedom Fighter**: strives for independence. They have been an employee in other businesses and decided to leave and start their own Endeavor. There is no one-size-fits-all freedom fighter, but you might be one if you've ever been a part of a system and thought, "I can do this better." It's the freedom fighter's constructive attitude that makes them so unique—and makes them perfect for a franchise system.

Whereas craftsmen and mountain climbers will have a strong desire to develop their own concept for a new business, freedom fighters are great fits for owning a franchise system; especially one that combines a framework for success with a lot of a flexibility.

The Freedom Fighter in the Franchise System

The freedom fighter is typically utilitarian and individualistic. They often feel that their managers don't know what they're doing and that they could do better. The following statements are reflective of the thoughts of a freedom fighter.

- They've often been sceptical about the decisions that the leaders of companies they worked for have made.
- They've felt frustrated that they don't have enough control over their career and their life.
- They may have believed that if they were in charge, they would approach things differently—and have a better outcome.
- They feel like their skills and their knowledge are often under-utilised by the businesses that they work for.
- They've had the thought in the back of their mind that they'd like to start their own business someday—so that they could benefit from running things their way.
- They've had the desire to have a greater impact in the world.

Success in Freedom

There are two types of franchise systems out there. One type is highly controlling; everything that they do must follow a precise, step-by-step process. For example, if they run a food-related franchise system, they cannot conceptualise new products or deserts, nor can they make variations on the set products. The store will look identical to any other franchise operator's. They need to operate within a very strict framework that allows zero creativity. This type of system is not too appealing to a freedom fighter.

What's so great about the freedom fighter, is that they can operate within a pre-existing system and make it fit their personal vision. They don't necessarily seek freedom from a system or guidelines, but freedom to work flexibly.

So, regardless of what your profile, if you're considering being a franchisee, make sure that you select the right franchise to suit you and check with the franchisor about the rigidity of their system.

For those of you considering becoming a franchisor, think about these three types of business owner in the context of the kind of franchisees that you would like in your system, and how you recruit them.

The franchisor needs to develop 'the six steps' of the 'people puzzle' and have systems for the franchisees just like an independent business owner would for their employees.

Takeaway

- ❖ You're in the people business regardless of what you sell.

- ❖ Understand the 'core needs' and the differences between owners, leaders, and employees, and what motivates them.

- ❖ Have a procedure for recruiting people into your business.

- ❖ Have a people management plan that addresses—induction, training, and performance management.

- ❖ Understand there are three types of potential business owner, and the need to recruit 'craftsman' or 'freedom fighters' for a franchise operation.

CHAPTER 9

FIND, KEEP & GROW
THE RIGHT CUSTOMER

Marketing & Sales

"Good marketing makes the company look smart. Great marketing makes the customer feel smart."

—JOE CHERNOV

MARKETING AND SALES

One of my clients has built a $10 million dollar business in just over 2 years with a marketing budget of just $200 per week, and next year their business will turnover more than $20 million dollars.

In the past 12 months, I generated more than $300,000 in sales from one activity with an expenditure of $1,200.

Both of these businesses have a marketing and sales strategy, and I think that a good place to start to understand how we did this, is to understand the process of marketing and sales. That is what we will cover in this chapter.

This topic is often referred to as 'sales and marketing', but I believe you have to put the activities in the right order, and marketing comes before sales. They are often intertwined or considered the same thing, but there is a clear distinction between the two.

The goal of marketing is to generate interest in a product or services, and for that marketing to generate leads or prospects. Marketing activities include:

- Consumer research to identify the needs of the customers.
- Product development—designing innovative products to meet existing or future needs.
- Advertising the products to raise awareness and build the brand.
- Pricing products and services to maximise long-term revenue.

On the other hand, sales activities are focused on converting prospects to actual paying customers. Sales involves directly interacting with the prospects to persuade them to purchase the product.

Marketing thus tends to focus on the broader population (or in any case, a large set of people), whereas sales tends to focus on individuals or a small group of prospects.

Peter Drucker famously wrote in *The Practice of Management* that the purpose of a business is to create and keep a customer, and while I agree with elements of this, I believe it goes further than that. I believe the purpose of business is to:

Find, Keep and Grow the Right Customer

The 'find' is where the marketing comes in, the 'keep' and 'grow' is where the sales process comes in, but by far the most important aspect of the marketing and sales process is ensuring that you have the 'right customer'. And this is a combination of both marketing to them, and sales; selling to them.

I love that saying by Henry Ford:

"Half the money I spend on advertising is waste, and the problem is I do not know which half."

While there is no guarantee that all of your marketing activity will work, there are ways to ensure it is more effective by talking to the right people about the right things. The way to do this is to clearly define who your ideal customer is, or who the modern day marketers refer to as your 'avatar' or 'buyer persona'.

So, let's explore how to define the right customer. To do this, there are a number of questions that you need to ask yourself:

- What is the gender, age and education of your target customer?
- What is their job?
- What is a day in their life like?
- What are their primary pain points?
- What do they value most and what are their goals?
- Where do they go for information?
- What is important to them in selecting a provider of your product or service?
- What are the most common objections?

I'd like to provide you with two examples as references to compare with. The first is with my business The Alternative Board. The second is with one of my Clients, Milky Lane, the business I referred to earlier that had $10 million turnover in just over two years with a marketing budget of $200 per week.

What both of us have done is define who our ideal customer is, what their problem, is and how we solve that problem.

The Alternative Board
The Alternative Board is the world's largest and most successful peer advisory and business coaching business, working with the owners of privately held businesses in the small to medium size market. So, let's look at how we defined our right customer.

The Alternative Board—Customer Profile

What is the gender, age and education of your target customer?

Both male and female business owners aged 25-60. The split of business ownership in Australia is heavily skewed to males at 69%.

What is their job?

Private business owners who offer services in the areas of: professional services like finance, legal, HR, recruitment, and other industry sectors in construction, retail, trade, service industry, wholesale trade, manufacturing, and distribution. We actually work across more than 300 industries.

What is a day in their life like?

Think about what an average day is like for them, who they deal with, and what affects their decision making.

A work day for a business owner is busy and constant. They need to juggle multiple tasks including managing staff. They work long hours and have the worry about securing new business to ensure positive cashflow.

They worry about the future and the responsibility towards their customers and their competition.

They know they need to have a strategic plan but don't have the time or knowledge to get started.

They are time poor and want to spend more time on the growth of the business versus the day-to-day tasks.

They want to be able to get enjoyment from owning and running their own business. Often they are technicians, good at their technical skill, and that is often what made them go into business, but it doesn't ensure that they will grow or be proficient in all aspects of running a business.

What are their primary pain points?
Try and describe the primary challenges they are trying to overcome that relate to your product or service

They feel alone with the challenges they face on a day-to-day basis running their business.

They want to take it to the next level and increase their profitability, but are unsure of the right way to go about it.

People management.

Time management—never enough time to get things done, owners work long hours, and over 50% of business owners work weekends and nights.

Cashflow and profitability.

What do they value most and what are their goals?
Try and explain what they value most when making a purchasing decision (price, service, support, etc.) and what they are trying to accomplish.

They know how to run their business, but they want to adapt the business so that it's less dependent on them.

They want to develop a culture within the business that drives their personal vision and provides a better work/life balance.

They need a strategic plan that is manageable and dynamic.

They want to recruit staff who will impact the business positively through increased productivity and profitability.

Being around other business owners; being a business owner is lonely

Where do they go for information?
Think about where they go to find information to make a purchasing decision (friend, Google, etc.).

The use the following platforms— Google, Facebook, LinkedIn, other social media, referrals from other business owners, their accountant, lawyer, family, and friends.

What is important to them in selecting a provider of your product or service?
Think about what is important when deciding between you and a competitor

They need to feel confident that they can be transparent when discussing their business in an open forum.

They want a trusted advisor who will lead from experience.

They want to be able to network and discuss their business challenges and successes with like-minded individuals.

They want to take their business to the next level and increase their productivity and profitability.

They want to attract and retain talented staff.

They want to develop a vision that creates a culture that delivers success.

They want to implement a strategic plan that is manageable, dynamic, and delivers results.

They want to make their business less dependent on them on a day-to-day basis.

What are the most common objections?
List the reasons you hear from potential customers as to why your product or service doesn't fit their needs

They are not ready to take that step—change is scary.

They may have a good business and don't feel that they need help.

They may have heard from people who have not had a good experience with business coaching.

The cost—they currently don't see the value, they just see the cost.

They do not understand the benefits of the insights and ideas of 4,000 business owners from all demographics, and the impact it could have on their decisions and business outcomes.

They don't have time to work on the business and step out of the day-to-day.

Milky Lane

Milky Lane was the brainchild of four young guys from Bondi Beach, who wanted to create a unique and complete experience that combines amazing food with art and great music. They provide a place where customers can enjoy world class and extreme burgers, desserts, and cocktails while listening to some hip hop or house music, and admiring the old-school street art throughout the venue.

Milky Lane—Customer Profile

What is the gender, age, and education of your target customer?

Milky lane appeals to a broad audience of both males and females, with a strong female skew of over 65%. The core target audience are aged between 18-35, but there are offerings for other age profiles including children. They are not ideal for older clientele or families with children.

A large proportion of their customer base is well educated and often very health and fitness focussed, so they understand food choices.

Milky Lane Customer Profile

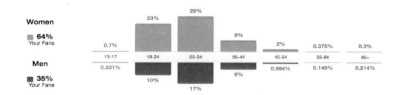

What is their job?
The majority of customers are a higher demographic with high disposable income and employed in professional services, and work primarily Monday to Friday, during the day.

What is a day in their life like?
They work hard in order to play hard; they enjoy eating out and experiences they can share with their friends. A significant proportion of the customers are active and attend the gym regularly.

What are their primary pain points?
They eat responsibly for the majority of the week and work hard in their roles, and on their diet and fitness, so they are often looking for an outlet and a way of spoiling themselves.

What do they value most and what are their goals?
Their customers value the relationships that they have with their friends and spending time with them. They live for now and want to celebrate life and their successes, and to reward themselves for their commitment to work, health, and fitness. They want to enjoy themselves and have fun.

Where do they go for information?
Social media is the key decider in determining where they go and spend their money. The influence of their friends and celebrities that also frequent the Milky Lane business

influences the desirability and aspirational nature of visiting Milky Lane.

What is important to them in selecting a provider of your product or service?

There is a significant number of similar operators offering food and beverages, but not many of them have wrapped it all up into a destinational, aspirational, and experiential hospitality venue. Customers want somewhere special that is differentiated from competitors. They want to be seen, and are happy to share that on social media for all their friends to know.

What are the most common objections?

The food is decadent and not something that you would eat every day. The restaurant is geared to a young cool vibe and may be a little intimidating to certain audiences. For some people, the music may be a little loud. The average price is mid-price point, so it is not cheap like some other burger operators.

Milky Lane knows who their customers are and who they want them to be, and every communication they have with them is about them. Too often, marketers get caught up in being creative and espousing the features of the business, product, or service. Milky Lane know it's about their right customer and what's important to them.

Once you have identified who your right customer is, you can then determine the best way to communicate with them and through what platforms.

There are commonly four accepted principles (Ps) of marketing, which includes product, place, price, and promotion. For businesses in the service industry, there are three additional Ps, which include physical environment, people, and process.

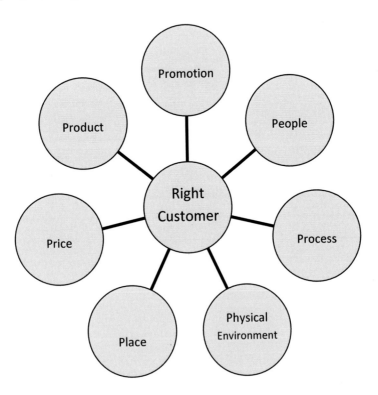

We have covered a lot of detail relating to people and process so far in this book. The others need to form part of your marketing strategy and plan.

The key to any marketing plan is to ensure that it is integrated and includes a combination of marketing activities.

There are marketing gurus out there, and much material written on how to market your business. I'm not going to attempt to compete with those experts, but wanted to share with you the principles and some key takeaways that non-marketers need to know to get the right advice from marketing professionals.

I want to focus on one aspect of marketing that is fast growing and much more measurable for the marketer and the business. Digital marketing consists of many elements and typically deals with **the** marketing efforts that use an electronic device or the Internet. Businesses need to leverage digital channels, such as search engines, social media, email, and their websites, to connect with current and prospective customers.

As such, companies today need to have a firm grasp on how to utilise the digital universe to maximise their brand awareness and impact.

I want to share with you two examples of digital marketing from the already identified businesses referenced earlier in this chapter: The Alternative Board representing a service based business, and Milky Lane representing a retail bricks and mortar business.

Both of these businesses have clearly identified who the right customer is for them, and once that has been done it is much easier to determine how you will communicate with those customers.

I have to admit, when I started my business, I was coming from ground zero. I had just left an extremely well paid job and paid a tidy sum to buy and set up my new business. So, I was keen to get customers, and at the time I didn't know who the ideal customer was. I admit to taking on anyone who would agree to use my services and pay me.

I knew about the 7 Ps and that I should be following them, but I was coming from a scarcity mode, and this caused me to make some poor decisions. My price point was low, and although I followed the established process, I made concessions that affected my growth and profitability in the early stages of my business. This prevented me from marketing effectively to the right customer.

Fast forward and my business is dramatically different. It's profitable, and the marketing activities that were generated in the first few years of operation are generating new business for me every day, often at no cost.

There were a number of activities that we did to build this momentum. Within our business we have a marketing strategy that we call IMAP, which stands for Integrated Member (Marketing) Acquisition Program. This program consists of 27 activities that we can undertake to market our opportunity. the 27 activities cross over 7 dimensions to ensure that we are not heavily reliant on just a few activities.

I wanted to share with you one activity that I undertook that generated in excess of $300,000 in sales in the past twelve months, at a minimal cost of $1200 plus my investment in time to generate the leads the activity generated for me.

That activity is perfectly designed for professional services sector or any business that is B2B, although it does have application for some B2C operators.

The activity that has generated this success for me is LinkedIn. I can remember back in the early 2000s when I first started receiving LinkedIn connection requests. I quickly dismissed it and thought it wouldn't take off. Well I was wrong. It has single handedly been the best marketing platform for my business. For most of my professional service and B2B clients, it has been the best of all the marketing activities that we have undertaken, and it's cheap to boot.

I'm still staggered that after starting in 2002, business people have not embraced this platform. I think there is some confusion about what it is and how to use to it as a marketing platform.

I'm not sure that I agree with some people's assertions that it is a form of a social networking, but for professionals. I believe that it is a network of some social interactions, but it's more about professional interactions, and focussed on professional networking rather than personal networking.
It has some elements of a social network, and there has been some change in how the platform has been used in recent times with the advent of the 'LinkedIn Local' phenomenon, where organisers encouraging people to share more about themselves personally. So, that it's not just about the person and their business profile. They are encouraging users to let people know who they are personally, as people tend to do business with people they know, like, and trust. There's no better way than giving people an insight into who you are beyond the business, professional background, and resume.

I don't believe that it's a lifestyle-oriented social network in the vein of Facebook, Instagram, or Google+. It's a platform for building a network of professionals with the goal of doing more business by engaging with the 'right people'.

We have used it to promote our position as thought leaders, to build a network of professionals, and ultimately find people who we can do business with.

Everyone should be on there, but invest in getting your profile right and use it actively, as it will result in lucrative dividends.

As a business owner the benefits are numerous, including:

- Joining relevant groups within your industry.
- Education and industry commentary.
- Generating leads with people that may need your products and services.
- Finding key employees; if they're on LinkedIn there's a strong chance they're open to discussion and in a lot of cases are more professional.
- If you're thinking about franchising your business, your prospects may be listed here.
- People like to do business with people they know, like, and trust. Often they will Google you and your company, and LinkedIn is really well optimised, making it easier to find you.

We have created a strategic approach to using LinkedIn to position ourselves within our category, and to engage with our target audience that is direct, responsive, and cost effective.

Milky Lane

I started working with Milky Lane when they had one store operating in early 2018. In 2019, they will open the tenth store and the store turnover will close in on $25 million. The boys who started the business, like most millennial and Gen Y business owners, had to bootstrap their business. Their marketing budget and expenditure was just $200 per week.

With a budget like that, you have to really know who your customer is and ensure that you talk directly to them. The most effective way for them to do this was through a digital marketing strategy, and specifically by using the social media platforms Facebook and Instagram.

In 2018, they were nationally recognised by The Optus MyBusiness Awards for Best Social media campaign, and their marketing director Christian Avant was recognised as the Australia Social Media Influencer of The Year. At the Awards evening, the owner of quite a large digital marketing agency came over to our table to congratulate Christian, as he has been able to do single handedly what significantly larger agencies have been unable to do. He commented to me, "I don't know how he does it, but he's bloody amazing."

To put this into perspective, let me share with you some of the incredible statistics that have been achieved through their social media strategy and activities.

On November 3, 2018 Milky lane launched a themed cocktail beverage based on the Bubble O 'Bill ice cream, and it was organically placed on Facebook.

It had a reach of 693,226 (unique people who saw the post). 143,738 Engagements (how many likes and comments were received, including likes/comments on the 2399 shares). 12k likes and 23k comments on the original post.

In late 2018 they had their content shared by some of the world's biggest viral pages with 2.2 million views on LadBible, 2.2 million views on FoodBible, and 2.3 million views on Business Insider.

In the first week of January 2019, they had 351,950 Instagram accounts reached with 1,535,455 impressions.

They have had greater reach and engagement than any other food business in Australia including McDonald's.

Quite simply, their business has been built on social media.

I am strong believer that marketers need to be authentic. Customers are way too smart these days and you'll be found out if you're not. Christian is truly authentic; he's not everyone's cup of tea, but what he does on social media is unparalleled. Not only is he authentic, but he's also very generous and in this section he shares his tips for building a successful, engaging Facebook and Instagram business account, and how to achieve significant organic reach that others can only ever dream of.

Facebook is constantly changing its algorithms, but as I write this section of the book, the last post Christian made this week on Facebook has over 1,200 comments without any expenditure, this result is totally organic. To put this in perspective, have a look at what your business's last post on social media achieved or better still think of the biggest brands you can think of and see what their organic comments are. I can guarantee that won't be anything like Milky Lane.

I haven't censored his language and vernacular; as I said earlier, it's all about being authentic and this is how Christian would tell you if he was sitting with you right now.

It's possible to achieve similar results if you follow Christian's tips:

1. Know your primary target audience and deliver content that they'd want to see. Over time it may end up being different to your original business plan but they're always #1. DON'T just continuously post what you want, post what THEY want.

2. Invest time, money, and research into creating the BEST CONTENT possible. A few pics on your iPhone with shitty lighting doesn't cut it anymore—find someone who specialises in your field/industry and the style of content you want, and plan the shoots meticulously so that you have an album full of killer material for that week or month.

3. Engage and chat with your followers. Every single person who leaves a comment on your posts is a chance to increase your reach, brand awareness, and online perception, etc. Listen to them and what they're saying, it's the best way to see what they really want. Ignoring them is basically saying, "I don't give a shit" and "I know best."

4. Be consistent. One good post and then 10 crap ones won't help you reach a greater audience in the long run. It takes a long while to build up an account that can achieve a large organic reach, most of which is done through consistently creating incredible content.

5. Give your brand a personality. Talk to your followers in a language they understand and BE REAL. "Hello and thank you for your message. Pls email XYZ and someone will be in touch" is SO ROBOTIC and displeasing. Don't be afraid to have a laugh, be cheeky, and ALWAYS BANTER. If there's a phrase that's red hot on the Internet right now, use that in your captions, etc.

6. Be current and on top of viral and or local trends. Sitting on what worked last year or even last month is a disaster waiting to happen. The core will always be the same, but there's constant changes or new things happening that you'll need to adapt to in order to be at the front.

7. Engage influencers to work with and support your brand. Whether it's a paid job (which we've never done yet), or a contra deal for food/drinks/clothing, etc., the power of these people on social media is VERY real. Look at the cost of the product to you that you're giving away, which is often quite small, and the potential return on that investment by generating even 10 new fans. A lot of companies say, "Why the hell should I give them something for free, that doesn't help pay my bills." If that's your mentality, you're in 2010 still and may as well retire.

"Some of you will skim this and think, "What does he know," and that's totally fine. I'm not a specialist with any supersized degrees etc., ha ha ha. But there are also a lot of people who ask how we manage to achieve thousands of organic comments on Facebook or 1.5 million impressions a week on Instagram."

The beauty of digital marketing and social media is the responsiveness and timeliness of anything that is posted; your audience sees it and comments on it instantaneously. Social media is the modern day secret shopper providing you feedback on your messaging and also your execution on your brand promise. So, if you get it wrong, you'll know about it and so will everyone else.

One thing that Christian does is comment to everyone that engages with Milky Lane on Social media. It amuses me if I like, comment, or share on their page, Christian engages and responds, so I always feel like they're listening.

With a clear digital and social media strategy your business will thrive.

I often get asked how much should a business be spending on marketing, and that's a really difficult question to answer without knowing answers to the following questions:

- What is the objective of your marketing activity? Is it to generate leads or to build the brand?
- What marketing activities have you done previously?
- Do you or have measured the financial returns of other marketing initiatives?
- What do you consider a fair return on your investment? It is commonly accepted that a $4 return for each dollar spent is desirable.
- Do you have a budget?

If you are able to answer those questions, the marketing can be more targeted.

My recommendations for business owners based on my experience, is that they should never stop marketing, as it is the continuity of activity that reinforces the brand in the consumers mind. And when they need your products or services, they will only remember you if you're communicating your products, services, and brand.

"The man who stops advertising to save money is like the man who stops the clock to save time."
—**Thomas Jefferson, 3rd American President**

New businesses need to spend at least 10% of their revenue initially and then this could settle at 5% of revenue. Franchise businesses typically collect between 2% to 3.5% of revenue, which goes into a marketing fund to be used for the benefit of the whole brand and network. One of the key attributes of a franchise business is the brand awareness that the franchisor has generated which enables them to spend a lower percentage of turnover on marketing, because of the longevity of the marketing activity and the buying power of having a bigger marketing budget.

We conducted some research with business owners that are members of The Alternative Board and asked them what they would do differently if they had their time over again, knowing what they know now back when they started their businesses. 38% of them said they would have spent more time marketing, and 35% of them said they wished they had spent more money marketing their business when they started it.

All this discussion on marketing is about 'finding the right customer' and generating interest in your products and services, and hopefully generating prospects and leads that will try your business. This is where the second part of the marketing and sales equation comes into play—sales.

Sales is what happens at the coal face, that moment of truth when the prospect tries your business and becomes a customer. A customer comes once but what every business needs is repeat business; we need customers to come back again and again and become clients.

Everything you do at an operational level will influence the 'keeping and growing the right customer', and that is why the processes and systems we discussed in chapter 7 are so important. Every business needs operational standards and a process for delivering service excellence.

Ray Kroc explained in his autobiography how he learned an important lesson:

"You could influence people with a smile and enthusiasm and sell them a sundae when what they'd come in for was a cup of coffee."

—Ray Kroc

Takeaways

❖ Find, keep and grow the right customer.

❖ Identify who the right customer is, what their problem is, where the congregate, and how you solve their problem.

❖ Are you marketing in the new millennium?

❖ Digital marketing platforms and a strong social media presence and marketing activity is critical.

❖ Have a marketing budget.

❖ Never stop marketing.

CHAPTER 10

SHOW ME THE MONEY

All Things Financial

"Beware of little expenses. A small leak will sink a great ship".

—Benjamin Franklin

All Things Financial

Poor Financial management led to the closure of one of my first clients. It devastated me and I felt like I should have done more. I should have known something was wrong when he wouldn't provide me with his P&Ls and balance sheet, and then when he sent me a cheque in the mail for his membership fees, I realised something wasn't right as all his other payments were direct debit.

This was a family operated business that had been operating for over 50 years with three generations of family members working in the business and 25 staff members all with families. This was a bad situation for everyone that could have been avoided with better financial management.

It was a salient moment for me, and it made me more vigilant in addressing the financial management of a business with all of the clients that I work with.

Setting up to be a successful business is no easy feat. It requires guts, hard work, and a good system, particularly when it comes to financial management. Running a successful business means that you now have even more responsibilities on your shoulders than you ever did as an employee. Your employees are dependent on you, and any decision that you take will not only affect you, but your team as well. Good leaders should always evaluate every decision they make with thought and caution, particularly when it involves handling business finances.

I want to start by talking about capital, and specifically the capital required to go into business. I can speak with experience about being undercapitalised myself. In a number of the franchise businesses that I worked in, franchisees were undercapitalised. It can have an impact on the business, and the mental and financial state of the business owners concerned.

Every business needs the capital to get started. The problem entrepreneurs and business owners, particularly the risk-takers, have is that they are optimistic and only see the best possible scenarios. They can often go into business undercapitalised by underestimating the true costs of operating, while overestimating the sales their business may generate.

The starting point for any business is the creation of a financial model and financial plan, and we referred to this as the business model in chapter 7. The business model can be broken into three parts to determine the financial requirements and decisions that need to be made:

1. **Cost of goods:** everything it takes to make something: design, raw materials, manufacturing, labour, and so on.
2. **Cost of sales:** everything it takes to sell that product: marketing, distribution, delivering a service, and processing the sale.
3. **Pricing and payment:** how and what the customer pays: pricing strategy, payment methods, payment timing, and so on.

Once you have determined the business model, which is how you are going to make money, you need to determine how much it is going to cost to establish the business. To do this, the business owner needs to create a financial modelling tool that combines the set up costs and the ongoing costs (cost of goods and sales) factoring in the pricing and payment strategy.

Now, you can build the financial model and see what it's going to take to get a return on your investment in time and money.

Here is an example of a financial forecast and income statement for my current business The Alternative Board.

INCOME STATEMENT - YEAR 1

	Mth 1 Apr-15	Mth 2 May-15	Mth 3 Jun-15	Mth 4 Jul-15	Mth 5 Aug-15	Mth 6 Sep-15	Mth 7 Oct-15	Mth 8 Nov-15	Mth 9 Dec-15	Mth 10 Jan-16	Mth 11 Feb-16	Mth 12 Mar-16	Year 1 Total
MEMBERSHIP COUNT													
Active members - Beg of month	0	0	0	12	12	13	13	17	22	22	21	22	0
New members added	0	0	12	0	1	1	5	5	0	0	1	1	26
Members lost	0	0	0	0	0	-1	-1	0	0	-1	0	0	-3
Active members - End of month	0	0	12	12	13	13	17	22	22	21	22	23	23
INCOME STATEMENT													
Revenues													
BAF Fees - avg fee of $500	-	-	6,000	-	500	500	2,500	2,500	-	-	500	500	13,000
Member Dues - avg due of $795	-	-	9,540	9,540	10,335	10,335	13,515	17,490	17,490	16,696	17,490	18,285	140,716
TAB additional opportunity income	-	-	1,017	1,017	1,102	1,102	1,441	1,864	1,864	1,780	1,864	1,949	15,000
Gross Revenues	-	-	16,557	10,557	11,937	11,937	17,456	21,854	19,354	18,475	19,854	20,734	168,715
Fees & Royalties paid to TAB													
Royalty Fee	-	-	3,311	2,111	2,387	2,387	3,491	4,371	3,871	3,696	3,971	2,275	31,872
Member Admin & Support fee - $10 per	-	-	120	120	130	130	170	220	220	210	220	230	1,770
Marketing Development fee	-	-	311	191	217	217	320	400	350	334	360	375	3,074
TAB Annual Conference Fee & FEE Fee	-	-	-	-	5,500	-	-	-	-	-	-	-	5,500
	-	-	3,742	2,422	8,234	2,734	3,961	4,991	4,441	4,239	4,551	2,881	42,216
Gross Margin	-	-	12,815	8,135	3,703	9,203	13,474	16,864	14,914	14,236	15,304	17,853	126,499
Expenses													
From Expense Assumptions page													
Marketing costs-other than Initial Campaign	-	-	-	-	300	300	1,500	1,500	-	-	300	300	4,200
Technology fee	First 3 mths are incl in initial invest			120	120	120	120	120	120	120	120	120	1,080
Automobile	600	600	600	600	600	600	600	600	600	600	600	600	7,200
Dues & subscriptions	100	100	100	100	100	100	100	100	100	100	100	100	1,200
Insurance - business, liability & auto	200	200	200	200	200	200	200	200	200	200	200	200	2,400
Office supplies & expenses	100	100	100	100	100	100	100	100	100	100	100	100	1,200
Professional fees	300	300	300	300	300	300	300	300	300	300	300	300	3,600
Travel, Meals & Entertainment	300	300	300	300	300	300	300	300	300	300	300	300	3,600
Telephone - Long distance & internet	200	200	200	200	200	200	200	200	200	200	200	200	2,400
Other Expenses - see "Expense Assum tab"	-	-	-	-	-	-	-	-	-	-	-	-	-
Loan Interest Paid	-	-	-	-	-	-	-	-	-	-	-	-	-
Amortization of Franchise Fee (non-cash)	1,192	1,192	1,192	1,192	1,192	1,192	1,192	1,192	1,192	1,192	1,192	1,192	14,304
	2,992	2,992	2,992	3,112	3,412	3,412	4,612	4,612	3,112	3,112	3,412	3,412	41,184
Net Profit (Loss)	(2,992)	(2,992)	9,823	5,023	291	5,791	8,862	12,252	11,802	11,124	11,892	14,441	85,315

Here is a summary of the financial returns including cash flow and profitability and some Key Performance Indicators (KPI's).

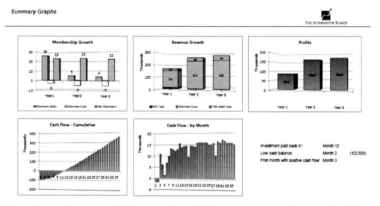

Summary Graphs

The financial modelling tool will demonstrate the cash flow and profitability and estimated return on capital based on the investment to establish the business.

To be profitable in business, it is important to know what your break-even point is. Your break-even point is the point at which total revenue equals total costs or expenses. At this point, there is no profit or loss—in other words, you 'break even'.

The formula is:

Break Even = _____ **Fixed Costs** _____
Point   **Total sales revenue – Cost to make product**
                          (Contribution Margin)

To better explain what all of this means, let's look at a breakdown of the formula components:

Fixed costs.
Fixed costs are not affected by the number of items sold. Fixed costs are required to be paid regardless of the sales generated. Examples include rent, fixed wages and salary, lease costs and loan repayments, contracts entered into, and legal and accounting costs. Fixed costs also include fees paid for services like graphic design, advertising, and PR.

Variable costs.
Variable costs are those that vary with sales, such as wages, utilities, and cost of goods and materials used in production of the finished product that is sold to customers.

Contribution margin.
The contribution margin is calculated by subtracting the variable costs from the selling price. Any money left after that represents your net profit.

Contribution margin ratio.
This figure is usually expressed as a percentage. It's calculated by subtracting your fixed costs from your contribution margin.

Profit earned following your break even.
Once your sales amount equals your fixed and variable costs, you have reached the break-even point.

To illustrate this exercise, let me share with you the break-even for one of my clients. They are a food franchise business.

Their weekly Fixed costs are:

Rent	$1,300
Wages	$3,200
Loan repayments	$1,000
Marketing	$ 500
Accounting	$ 200
Total Fixed costs	**$6,200**

Their weekly Variable costs are:

Food & Packaging	$4,000
Casual wages	$ 500
Utilities	$ 300
Office Expenses	$ 200
Operating supplies	$ 200
Miscellaneous costs	$ 400
Total Variable Costs	**$5,600**

$$\frac{\text{Fixed costs} = \$6,200}{\textbf{Sales} \ (\$20,000) \ - \ \textbf{Costs} \ (\$5,600) = \$14,400}$$
(Contribution Margin)
Contribution margin % = 57%
Break-even point = $11,800 per week in sales

The business starts to make profit on every dollar over the break-even sales of $11,800. Once a business owner knows their break-even sales, they can focus on sales building activities and controlling costs accordingly.

When starting a business and completing a break-even analysis, much of it is based on assumptions and projections unless you are part of an established business model like a franchise system. This is one of the many benefits associated with franchising: the fact that it is a proven model perfected over time and should provide the business owner with a more accurate estimate of income and expenses.

Either way, the break-even analysis should be completed regularly, as should the contribution margin, as this will help you analyse the profitability of products and assist in determining the ideal price or continued viability of a product.

In rough terms, the contribution margin ratio will give an indication of the likely percentage of additional revenue that drops to the bottom line as profit. Knowing this can be quite motivating and assist the business owner in making good decisions.

If you need to get money from a finance company, you will need to complete a business plan which includes the business model and the break-even analysis. The creation of a budget and cash flow forecast is essential for financiers to consider your application. But even more important is factoring any borrowings into your forecasts and knowing that you have the ability to service the debt, and what the finance does to your break-even and profitability.

My Mistakes

When I started all of my businesses, I did all the bookkeeping and accounting work myself. Not content with working fulltime and between six and seven days a week, I would do my bookkeeping on the lounge in front of the television at night. I would drive my wife mad.

Many business owners start doing their own books, and there are definite benefits to doing this, as it enables you to manage the cash coming in and going out (cashflow) and gives you a good handle on the business. Some of us think we are saving money by doing it ourselves, but it's a bit of a false economy, because often we're not good at it, and we resent it and what it does to our free time. Often it takes us much longer to do than a professional, and sometimes we get it wrong. Thankfully, there are some fantastic accounting software systems available now that make it much easier to manage your books.

Sound bookkeeping is the basis for all financial management. It is really important to set things up correctly from the start and get the professional advice that you need. I have to admit to doing it cheaply by doing it myself, and not having the right accountant to advise me. Fast forward four years, and I have had to go back and fix it, and it has cost me thousands of dollars to get it right and set it up properly. So, my strong advice is to invest in the finance function early on, and as soon as you can afford to, engage a good bookkeeper to do your bookkeeping work.

Get a strong financial advisor to help you set up and to advise you. I used cheap services, and here's the thing with cheap: it's just not good value. This year, I spent double what I should have because I had to get work redone. Pay a little bit more for the right person.

It is worth engaging a strong finance person to create all of your finance set up functions including, chart of accounts, accounting software and set up, budgets, cash flow forecasting, break-even analysis, and to help develop your business model.

Once you're up and going make sure that you complete monthly P&Ls and cash flow forecasts. A profit and loss (P&L) statement is the best tool for knowing if your business is profitable, and a cash flow statement will help you know what's coming and what to plan for.

Each month, you should analyse your P&L and create an action plan to improve areas of opportunity. But don't wait till the end of the month, as by then it will be too late. You need to establish Key Performance Indicators (KPI's) that you measure every day, and those that you measure every week so that you can adjust course if need be.

"You can't manage what you can't measure."

—Peter Drucker

When I was at McDonald's, we measured everything. Sometimes we measured the ridiculous; we used to determine our yields, which meant how many finished servings we received for a raw ingredient. A good example of why I say it was ridiculous was because we measured our French fry yield (how many servings of fries per 100kg of raw product) by counting the number of fry bags and boxes. The reason this was crazy, was because of waste and the sheer number of fry bags and boxes we had in store, and the potential for errors. This resulted in huge variances.

A smarter way to measure was to determine how many French fries went into a serve by dividing the number of serves sold through the cash register system by the weight of fries used. This showed you whether you were getting the optimum number of finished goods from the raw ingredients used. The McDonald's fry yield was 840 to 880 small servings per 100kg. If you got less servings, you may have been overfilling bags or had bad controls. If you got a higher yield, then potentially customers weren't getting the correct sized serving. Knowing this information enabled you to go and observe operations, and see where the problem was so you could do something about it.

Every product at McDonald's had a yield to enable them to measure the profitability of the production processes.

One of the other key measurements at McDonald's was determining the optimum cost of producing a product, versus the actual cost achieved in the production of the product.

For example, a cheeseburger had a range of raw ingredients: bun, meat patty, mustard, ketchup, pickle, and a slice of cheese. The process to determine the food cost of making the cheeseburger was adding all the raw costs. Back when I worked there, the cost was around 40¢, and we sold the burger for $1.60 resulting in a food cost of 25%.

If all we sold was cheeseburgers, and we sold 1,000 of them, our sales would be $16,000 and our costs should have been $4000, so our optimum cost of raw ingredients would be 25%. If the actual cost of what we bought was less, then either we had a stocktaking error, or we weren't putting the right amount of ingredients on the burger (some stores had one pickle days, which saved money—this was non-sanctioned). If the actual food cost was higher than 25%, then we had an operational problem and our control measures weren't in place. Our allowed variance was 0.3% and stores that had good controls were able to achieve this.

The reason for describing this scenario is that every business needs to know what the optimum cost of production should be, and determine what it actually is. If there is a variance, you need to investigate the reasons—that's good financial management.

In order to do that, you need to have a strong financial model. Your budget will be your roadmap for financial success, and the KPI's and P&L reports will be your measurement. It's important to know what industry benchmarks are and how you compare. This information is easy to find online and if you're in a franchise system, chain of operators, industry, or considering becoming a franchisor, then you will have other similar businesses to use as the benchmark.

When I worked in a very large recruitment business, we made it a requirement that our franchise owners maintained three months' working capital, and they had to provide us with a statement each month to verify this. We did this because of the nature of that industry, but also because it was just good practice. If you have three months of working capital (your break-even costs), you can confidently make investment decisions that don't compromise the cashflow of the business.

With all of the business owners I work with, I instil the need to have three months' working capital, especially if they are thinking of investing in additional resources or products as this mitigates risk.

I currently have two clients who have included the full financial function into their franchise business model. They do everything for the franchisee, and in doing so have the systems set up and streamlined for efficiency. This enables the franchisee to focus on the core operations without the distraction of the finance function. And for the franchisor, they know exactly where each franchisee is with cash flow and profitability, and are able to react quickly if help is needed.

Good financial management is the key to the success of every business, but in particular a franchise system.

Good financial management results in a better return on investment (ROI). Here is a rough guide:

- Businesses under $100,000 may take 12 to 24 months.
- Businesses from $180,000 to $400,000 may take 2.5 to 3.5 years.
- Businesses from $500,000 to $850,000 may take around four years.
- Businesses over $1m may take five or more years.

For those considering franchising as a model for growth or business entry, franchisees typically spend seven years in a network which, if they are successful, allows them to realise ample goodwill value upon the sale of their business.

Good financial management enables better financial performance and a cleaner set of books. This is particularly important when it comes time to sell. I know from experience that the better the books, the better the controls, and the better the profitability. This results in a better valuation and a quicker sale of the business.

Every business will sell, so preparing for it is a must. Get the right advice, set your financial plans and controls up correctly from the start, and create financial disciplines evert day, week, and month. The more efficient and effective you are at the start, the easier it will be throughout and at the end.

<u>Takeaways</u>

- ❖ Create a business model that enables profitability.

- ❖ Create a budget and cashflow forecast.

- ❖ Determine your break-even.

- ❖ Have three months of working capital in reserve.

- ❖ Establish KPI's and measure regularly.

- ❖ Invest in a good accountant—you get what you pay for.

- ❖ Set up your accounting systems properly from the beginning.

- ❖ Complete regular P&Ls and action plans.

CHAPTER 11

THE MODERN DAY BUSINESS COACH

Hear From Some Industry Experts

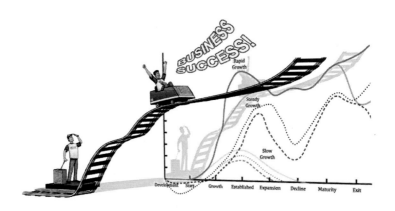

"One of the greatest values of mentors is the ability to see ahead what others cannot see and to help them navigate a course to their destination."

—John C. Maxwell

Why the Best Coach May Not Be a Coach at All

In my current business, The Alternative Board, we regularly conduct research and poll hundreds of entrepreneurs, asking them whose advice they trust most when faced with critical issues affecting their business. The most recent survey we conducted on this topic revealed that entrepreneurs put the most faith in the advice of fellow business owners (31%)—more than business coaches (24%) or consultants (4%). Additionally, when entrepreneurs do hire a business coach, 73% seek out someone who has owned their own business.

75% of business owners face the same challenges, regardless of size or industry. With fellow business owners ranking as the single-most trusted advisor, it's clear entrepreneurs are seeking advice from someone who is current, in-the-field, and whose motivation for giving advice isn't personal or professional gain.

It is for this reason that I reached out to the business leaders and business owners who inspire me and have made an indelible mark on the people, businesses, and sectors, including franchising here in Australia.

I have played around with who do I put first, I tried to rank them, but the reality is that they are all impressive leaders, and all have something memorable and worthwhile to share with the broader business community. Trying to allocate position in this chapter was like picking between your children and reminds me of the biblical tale in the 'Judgement of Solomon'.

I believe you will find nuggets of gold in the following chapter; principles that you can adopt into your own business to create similar levels of success that the contributors to this chapter have done in their careers and businesses.

PETER RITCHIE

Peter Ritchie trained as an accountant and worked for a firm of chartered accountants while at university. From 1966-1969, he worked in London for the International Wool Secretariat, and for a firm of management consultants. Returning to Sydney, he managed a property development company before being approached in 1970 to join McDonald's and train in the United States.

Peter was the first employee of McDonald's Australia and the first employee of the McDonald's system outside North America. During the 70's and 80's, he played a major role in every aspect of the company's development.

McDonald's Australia grew to more than 500 stores and 50,000 employees during his time as Chief Executive.

In 1983 and 1991, he was a member of the Board of the US parent company, McDonald's Corporation, and helped establish McDonald's in most of the countries in Asia and the Pacific, including Hong Kong, Singapore, Malaysia, Indonesia, and New Zealand. He was a founding Board Member of McDonald's Hong Kong, Malaysia, and New Zealand.

In December 1995, Peter announced his retirement from an executive role at McDonald's Australia after 25 years with the company. Peter was non-executive Chairman of the Board from 1995 until his resignation in December 2001.

Peter's executive positions have included Chairman of Mortgage Choice Australia Limited, Chairman of Reverse Corp Limited, Chairman of Culligan Australia Pty Limited, and Deputy Chairman of the Seven Network Limited.

To top it off, Pete is down to earth, humble, and an all-round great bloke.

I had the great privilege to spend a morning with Peter Ritchie to interview him for this book, and he proceeded to answer all of the same questions that the other contributors have commented on. But we were able to go even deeper, and I had the opportunity to spend time asking him about his experiences with McDonald's. Pete gave me some great insight into the early days in the USA and Australia, and deeper insight into key McDonald's leaders like Ray Kroc and Fred Turner.

I came away from my meeting with Pete with my (heart and head) glass full to the brim.

What was even more of a treat was hearing stories about the early days of McDonald's in the USA. I have done a lot of reading about the McDonald's early days. I also lived through a good portion of Peter's leadership and got to experience the business under his direction, but to get Peter's insight and real-life experiences really put things into perspective for me.

I enjoyed watching the movie 'The Founder' and asked Pete if it was a fair representation of the McDonald's story. Pete said it was, but it primarily focused on Ray Kroc and dealt mainly with the period up to the early 1960s. Pete shared with me that Fred Turner was instrumental in the development of the McDonald's brand, and he did not get too much coverage in that movie. Pete holds Fred in very high regard.

Pete said he had two great mentors at McDonald's in the early days: Fred Turner and Don Wilson. Fred was like Pete, while Don had a very different set of skills than Pete. Don was detail oriented and was in fact the first (Dean) head of Hamburger University. It was him who influenced on Pete of the importance of training.

I have some key takeaways that I received from my time with Pete, which I wanted to share with you. A couple of these were things I recalled from things he said back in the 1990s. They were reinforced for me spending this time with him during our catch up.

I found it amazing that as we talked about McDonald's, Pete kept referring to being part of the business in the present tense, and saying 'we' when he spoke about it. It was like he was still part of the business, but Pete retired in 2001. This is symptomatic of anyone that worked in a business for a long period of time, but speaks of the culture that Pete instilled into the business, and anyone that spent any time at McDonald's knows that feeling.

We got talking about family partly, because McDonald's was a family but also because business can impact on family. My takeaway from this discussion was that it's important to create a culture of family among your team, but remember your family is everything. Don't sacrifice them for the business— the business doesn't really care how hard you work and as Pete said to me 'no meeting is so important that you can't miss it'.

Q. Why should business owners should think and behave like franchisors?

It forces you to be disciplined to set up systems, with an emphasis on being disciplined in your approach to everything that you do. You need to document and put things in writing, so your people can read and understand the standards.

Fred Turner wrote the original operations manual, and it was still evolving when I joined McDonald's. They hadn't expanded into international markets and were really feeling their way. This was good for me as I pretty much had carte blanche to run the business the way I wanted.

We got to 85 stores, and franchises were making good money, but the QSC standards were not where I wanted them to be. Although I knew the importance of training, I wasn't yet the advocate I later became. I wanted to operate the best McDonald's business globally, and I took the senior management team around the world to benchmark international standards. I was blown away by the Singapore operations. My senior management team pointed out to me the number of staff they had on the floor, and that made it easier for them, because the labour rates were significantly lower than the Australian market.

In order to become the best McDonald's operation in the World, we invested even more heavily in our people. Our plan was to create a culture of true commitment to training, and in 1986 we invested 30% of our bottom line profit back into systemwide training initiatives.

This investment in training dramatically impacted our productivity and we were ranked in the bottom 2% globally. But within five years we were ranked number one in the world and McDonald's Australia continue to be ranked number one in the McDonald's world.

My advice is to invest in people and training. "Training doesn't cost, it pays."

Q. What lessons did you learn from franchising?

Franchising is not for everyone, as it's a constant push and pull between the franchisor and the franchisee. Especially early on in the relationship, it can be a struggle. Most people don't like confrontation, but there are benefits from the clash of strong personalities as long as it is done respectfully.

If you have a franchisee who gets into your system and they are not the right fit, you need to recognise it early and get them out of the system before they cause trouble across the system. I made the mistake of not taking issue early enough and letting the wrong people stay in the business too long before we took action.

Q. *What are your top three pieces of advice for business owners?*

Don't get into, it or stay in it, if you are not wholeheartedly focused on the business. Business requires total focus, so you can't be in it part-time.

Ensure that the margin is factored into your business model. Profit needs to be there but not immediately.

Q. *What are your top three pieces of advice for aspiring franchisors?*

I only have one piece of advice—make sure there is enough profit for both franchisees and the franchisor. There are too many franchise systems where this isn't the case. Both parties need to make more than just a living; they need a return on their capital investment and their time, and be rewarded for their effort.

Q. Any other business advice you would like to share?

If you think franchising will work for your model, then open a number of stores yourself and prove it with them, then decide if franchising is the right business model to use.

You need to be aware of your market and the sector you are in. Is there a need for your product and how big is the market opportunity?

You need to build up volume in order to enter the mass market, and if there is enough volume this may be a reason to franchise.

Don't spread your brand and business too quickly, as you need to keep your eye on the business so you can react quickly.

RAY ITAOUI

I met Ray Itaoui back in 1993 when he was promoted from McDonald's crew member into a trainee manager role, and he was working for my wife who was his store manager. She's a strong manager with high standards, and she helped ensure that Ray learnt things the right way. I know Ray appreciated her stern hand, and she has high standards that I can attest to. She used to come home and tell me stories about this amazing trainee manager who she had, named Ray.

Ray worked with Lisa for a few years and progressed right through to managing one of the highest volume stores in the country, taking over from Lisa. You could see that Ray was driven, ambitious, and people oriented, and that he would go a long way. Unfortunately, the opportunities didn't present themselves at McDonald's and Ray left to join Sanity Music as an area manager.

I've followed Ray's career from afar. I used to bump into him in airports as we both travelled around Australia. I was always hugely impressed by him, and even more so by his achievements in recent years. The thing that strikes me about Ray is how hard he works and just how humble he is. When I asked him to contribute to this chapter of the book, he essentially said, "I'm not sure why you want me, I'm not worthy." I ask you to judge for yourself after reading about his success and his advice for business owners on the following pages.

Ray joined Sanity in 2001 on a much lower salary than other roles were offering, as he saw the huge opportunity. He started as an area manager and worked his way up to Queensland state manager. He turned around that state's stores and later was promoted to national manager. In 2007, Itaoui become Sanity's chief executive officer.

Turning $500,000 into $210 million

The Sanity business hit some hard times, and the then current owner Brett Blundy had made a decision to sell or close that division of his businesses. He let Ray know, and it was a hard thing for him to take. He was used to winning and being successful, and the Sanity business wasn't doing so well, when all of Brett's other businesses were performing really well.

Ray decided there had to be an option for Sanity other than closure, and he offered to take the chain off Blundy's hands for nothing. In return, he would take on the losses and the risk of trying to turn it around.

"Brett thought I was insane," recalls Ray. "We had a debate about it. It was more about him making sure I knew what I was getting myself into. I said, 'Mate, I get it. You've got eighteen million to lose, I don't.'"

In fact, Ray had plenty to lose. He had a $500,000 stake in Sanity, two mortgages, and worse, he had put the plan forward without consulting his wife. "She cracked it," he said. Ray hadn't wanted to be talked out of his plan. So he put the plan into place and took control of the ownership of Sanity.

Quickly, he set about fixing the business. Sanity's profitable stores were mostly in regional areas, so he shut around 100 stores and pared the business back to 156 outlets that now stretch from Karratha to Echuca.

"One of the things that kept me awake at night after the change of ownership was, 'I'm going to take these guys from working with a god-like figure and they're going to be very disappointed that the new owner is a nobody.'"

After laying out a strategy, Ray set targets, which if met meant all of his 60 managers would get a trip to Fiji. Guess what? They did.

He introduced an annual gala event for his teams, and the first event featured Delta Goodrem and Guy Sebastian performing.

Ray's focus was on outstanding customer service "We want the customer for life, we don't want it to be just a $30 transaction," he said.

"We genuinely treat our team like they're family and we want that replicated back to the customer. To have a real connection and bond with the customer, that is unique, that you're not going to get elsewhere."

The transition to a board director role was an adjustment for Ray, who says he got a personal coach to help with the move from being an executive in control to a business owner. He says the coach also helped him become comfortable with his wealth.

Q.   What lessons did you learn from franchising?

As a CEO, if you'd asked me did I treat the business as if I owned it, I would've said 'Absolutely. 100%.' I always felt I treated the business as my own. But once I went from CEO to owner of the business, I quickly realised the reality. Yes, I ran the business like it was my own, but it's not the same as being an owner.

One of the things I learnt very quickly as an owner, is that cash is more important than profit. While I understand, yes profit is cash … you can still spend more than your profit on more stock than you need, or over capitalising on a fit-out, or buying unnecessary equipment. These can all drain your cash very quickly and put you in a troubling position. For this reason, I have never been a fan of debt (or too much debt). With borrowings, it's easier to spend on things that are unnecessary.

Each week, Ray has a weekly cash flow report run to ensure the cash flow is forecasted for the three months in advance. It's a very important practice and puts things into perspective very quickly.

Q. What are your top pieces of advice for business owners?

Support—have people around you who can give you advice. It is essential to ensure that regardless of what you're doing. If you haven't done it before, find someone who has. Learn from their mistakes. You will be surprised just how many people are willing to take the time and share their learnings with you.

For this reason, I joined YPO (Young Presidents Organisation). In my chapter, there are 90 people from all different industries, who have been there and done it before. If I am stuck or about do something I have little experience in, I reach out to someone who has it, who can share their learnings. YPO may not always have the relevant advice though. For example, if I am in a regional town or in a shopping centre and I need advice, I will talk to the local people. There is always someone to learn from.

If you're buying a franchise, you need to find someone who has done it before … there is no shame in asking for help. For example, if you're thinking about investing in a Subway franchise. Find three stores that are in a similar demographic, in a similar environment as your potential store, i.e. in a major shopping centre, or is it in an industrial area, then reach out to the owner. Find out as much information as you can from them—what would they do differently? What do they wish they did and didn't do? What has been their biggest mistake? What caught them by surprise? These are just some questions you could ask them, and while some of these questions may seem negative, they are the type of questions you could learn from.

If you're signing a new lease in a shopping centre, do your research—ask around. How much are other retailers paying per sqm? What is their lease term? How much contribution did they receive towards their fit-out?

Take the time to ask before doing—there is no shame in learning from others.

Have a vision ... and take your team on the journey. To achieve outstanding results, you first need to know where you're heading. And more importantly, so do the team that work for you. What is it you want the future to look like? If it's a single store, do you want to be the best store in the country? Or do you see yourself having 20 stores, or 100 stores?

Once your vision is clear, you need to set your goals and have your team set goals. Setting goals and then putting an action plan for each of the goals in place will ensure you stay on track to achieve them and keep your team focussed on the outcome.

It's important to constantly revisit your vision. Are your goals going to help you achieve the vision you have set? Are the action items getting you closer to your goals?

Each year I set new goals, professionally and personally. Each goal is articulated in broad terms and then fleshed out in more detail.

Not all my goals are huge items that need a lot of work. They are, however, important enough for me and without the proper focus will not be completed.

People—Master the Art of Managing people

No matter what line of business you're in, your success or failure will ultimately come down to the strength and weaknesses of your people. If you haven't already, you will quickly learn there is only so much you can do by yourself to influence your business results.

People management starts at the recruitment stage. Before you recruit anyone, you really need to think about what kind of person you actually want. What kind of team member are you looking for? A lot of time, money and effort is wasted if this part is not taken seriously. The right person can make all the difference to the success of your business, while adversely, the wrong person can be extremely detrimental.

Managing people is an art form and takes a lot of practice, but it really is easy. I learnt from a very young age at McDonalds, "Treat people like you want to be treated," which in 90% of situations is correct. However, you need to ultimately accept that everyone who you work with is different and will need to be treated differently. It's essential to get to know your people and figure out how you get the best out of each individual. You need to learn how to be tough, fair, genuine, and caring all at the same time.

In addition to this, it's important to make time for your people—proper sit down time. I have a rule in my businesses, that everyone should have a one-on-one meeting with their direct report for approximately 45-60 minutes each week.

Challenge yourself and others around you to continually grow. I have been a business owner for the last 10 years, and for the 5 years prior to this, I was the CEO of Sanity/Virgin/HMV with 300 stores and an annual turnover of over $300 million. Despite this, I still today genuinely believe that I have so much more to learn. I am always looking at ways to be more productive, to be a better leader, or even a better husband and father. Personally, I try to do one international education course per year to help me become a more effective leader, and the books I read are business related, or books that will teach me something.

One of the biggest issues businesses should try to avoid is complacency. It's important to acknowledge that everything can always be done better, and be prepared to challenge everything you do to find ways to improve. Once you're looking for ways to improve, the people around will do the same. Part of this is not being afraid to come out of your comfort zone. Remaining in your comfort zone is no doubt the easiest option, but I don't believe you can achieve what you're capable of, or be truly satisfied unless you're willing to do this.

CATRIONA NOBLE

Catriona rose through the ranks at McDonald's and became Australia's first female CEO at the ripe old age of 40. During her 20 year career, there she held the CEO and Managing Director role of the Australian business, and was Chief Restaurant Officer for Asia, Pacific, Middle East, and Africa.

In that role, she was responsible for more than 10,000 restaurants and 200,000 people. Catriona earned a reputation as an innovator in driving cultural change to achieve success. She is a member and mentor with the Business Council of Australia and a member of the Australian Social Inclusion Board, of which she is the Deputy Chair of the National Place Based Advisory Group.

I worked for Catriona for a few years in the training department at McDonald's but knew of her for a long time before, and after, and I knew that Catriona would be whatever she wanted to be. She had the drive, intelligence, and passion to be successful at whatever she put her mind to. The press shares her prowess in the two behemoth companies she worked for, but she also understands small business, as her family has owned at least four businesses that I know of.

She left McDonald's after more than 30 years and joined a totally different industry in banking, and what she describes of those feelings is reflective of the feelings of all business owners: "It's about creating an atmosphere of stretch, nervousness, and stepping towards your fears rather than suppressing them."

Catriona joined ANZ in 2015 as Managing Director Retail Distribution, responsible for the bank's key retail distribution channels which include the Australian Branch Network, Mobile Lending, Brokers, and Customer Contact Centre, along with the management of ATMs. She is a key member of the Australia Division Leadership team, and a member of the Australian Risk Committee.

Q. *Why should business owners think and behave like a franchisor?*

The rigours of being a franchisor require you to create a level of discipline and process excellence that is easily repeatable, and internal benchmarking capability to an exceptional level. Quite simply, you must build a well-oiled machine and constantly innovate to ensure it is market leading.

Q. *What lessons did you learn from franchising?*

Don't be in franchising unless you believe in the magic of it. Franchisees can create a lift in business performance that cannot be formulaically identified through a mutually beneficial and interdependent relationship. In McDonalds, this is known as the three-legged stool, the third being the suppliers, and the stool cannot stand unless all three legs are in balance.

Q. *What advice would you give to aspiring franchisors?*

Treat franchisees as business people, not employees. Ensure the remuneration level reflects this, but also don't protect them from every risk or the vagaries of the business cycle.

Understand the pros and cons of franchising. Franchisees are accountable for their own business and are entrepreneurs, but also have an interdependency with the franchisor that at times requires them to align with the system and brand even when they may not agree. Go in with your eyes wide open; the symbiotic nature of the relationship does not work without this mutual understanding.

Don't think this is just an easy way to access capital or hire glorified employees who have no limit to their working hours. Franchising requires a mutual respect and a sharing of the 'power' in the relationships. Both parties must feel they have a vested interest in making the right choices for themselves and each other.

PETER DAVIS

Peter Davis is one of Two Australian franchisors to make the SeoSamba's Top 100 Global Influencers in Franchising list. This list includes the most influential characters in the franchise world, and we are fortunate to have Peter as a contributor to this chapter. Peter is an outstanding and successful business owner and franchise professional.

Peter was in the Royal Australian naval college for seven years, before joining the NSW Fire Brigade and completing a Bachelor of Arts Degree.

Peter is the Managing Director and Franchisor for Frontline Recruitment Group. Frontline operates Industry and Geographic specific recruitment Agencies specialising in Retail , Hospitality, Health, Education, and Construction sectors in locations across Australia and New Zealand.
With over 20 years of success and experience in the recruitment industry, Peter has partnered in and helped start over 40 recruitment agencies in many different industry sectors, locations, and market conditions.

Traditionally, Frontline established and then franchised agencies to business partners, and have more recently created an innovative 'partnering program', which is a uniquely flexible opportunity to enable prospective franchisees to own their own business, when ordinarily they may not have the financial capacity to do so. Peter believes if they are the right person, then you should remove the barriers to entry and create an opportunity that works for the franchisor and franchise partner.

I worked with Peter for a few years, and I count on him as a friend and mentor for me in my business.

Q. *Why business owners should think and behave like a franchisor?*

For the purposes of answering this question, lets remove the legalities of franchising and look at the underlying behaviours of successful franchisors and focus on those.

At its core franchising is about partnering … the franchisor and the franchisee are business partners, and like all partnerships there are good times and bad.

Business owners are partners … the partners will be the clients and the suppliers. If it is a big business there will also be Shareholders who are partners. If it is a family business there will be other family members. We do not usually refer to clients, suppliers, shareholders, and family members as partners, but they are and working with them, through good times and bad, is a key to the success of any business.

Q. *What lessons did you learn from franchising?*

Key lesson: the business is owned by the people in it … in a franchised business, it is the franchisees who are the 'beating heart' of the business. The franchisor may be the brains behind the business, but the heart is the most important part.

Q. *What are your top three pieces of advice for business owners?*

1. Years 1-5: learn to live on toast and vegemite because you may not be able to afford much else.
2. Businesses are long term … If you don't truly love what you are doing you won't last the distance.
3. Your business is your cash flow vehicle behind which you build your personal wealth.

Q. What are your top three pieces of advice for aspiring franchisors?

1. Stick to your business system, stay focused on what you know works, and don't change your system if it does not work for everyone.
2. After your franchise partners have learnt to operate your system effectively, recognise that the issues that will affect their franchise will most likely be a result of changing personal circumstances. Get to know them personally so you can support them personally.
3. Franchisees are generally conservative (otherwise they would not be attracted to franchising), so change takes time… and consultation… this means franchisors always need to be thinking two to three years ahead

Q. Any other business advice you would like to share?

For aspiring business owners: surround yourself with people who are smarter and or more experienced than yourself … and then (metaphorically) partner with them!

JASON ZICKERMAN

Jason joined The Alternative Board (TAB) in May 2001 as the Executive Vice President and Chief Operating Officer. He became a member of the Board of Directors on April 1, 2002. In January 2004, he assumed the role of TAB's President and Chief Operating Officer. He remained the Chief Operating Officer until November 2008, when he assumed the role of Chief Executive Officer. Jason also received the Samba top 100 franchise influencers in the world in 2018.

Jason sustains an exceptional knowledge and passion for business, combined with strategic counsel and astuteness that fuels the success of organisations. His expert counsel is consistently recognised throughout the world's most influential media, including BusinessWeek, CNN, CFO, Forbes, The Wall Street Journal, The Globe and Mail, Investor's Business Daily, MSNBC, The Associated Press, Smart Money, and Reuters. Multiple appearances on Fox Business News are due to the real-world value and timeliness of advice as an authority on issues faced by small-to-medium businesses.

Jason has led the TAB business to become the world's largest for-profit peer board and coaching services organisation, with franchise businesses operating in more than 20 countries and having helped in excess of 20,000 privately owned businesses in that time.

I met Jason in 2004 when I acquired the Master Franchise rights for The Alternative Board in Australia. Jason has been my personal coach and mentor since then, and is someone I consider not only an outstanding business leader and Franchisor, but also a good friend.

Q. Why should business owners think and behave like a franchisor?

The key benefits of behaving like a franchise are significant. In a franchise system, one of your key goals is to be able to provide a repeatable process that is clear and concise, as well as easy for others to follow. If done correctly, the business will prosper.

When a business reviews its systems and processes to evaluate whether or not it is clear on what to do and what to avoid, it will force that business to make improvements as well as question what and why they are doing things they are currently doing. By going through this integral process, the organization will ultimately become more efficient and excel, because you will be forced to tighten up your processes and systems. Besides running a better business due to providing your employees and other stakeholders with a clear understanding of their roles, the training and on-boarding of your employees also becomes significantly stronger.

Not deviating from your documented systems and processes allows you, as well as others, to have confidence that no important information has been omitted. This will also massively help in the sale of your business at the appropriate time.

One of the biggest concerns to a buyer of a business is how dependent they are on the owner and his or her institutional knowledge, as well as how vulnerable they are at losing key employees. Will they lose the know-how at their departure? You will significantly reduce this risk having your systems and processes well documented.

Q. *What are your top three pieces of advice for business owners?*

1. Know your differentiation in the market place

2. Run your business by focusing on key KPIs (key performance indicators). This will tell you most of the story you will need in order for you to run your business.

3. Never try to be efficient when it comes to relationships. Don't forget at the end of the day, in almost all cases, business will come down to people.

Q. *What are your top three pieces of advice for aspiring franchisors?*

1. Organise all of your processes and systems to an incredibly high level of detail so others can have confidence following your system.

2. It's all about unit economics. If your unit franchisees are happy and successful, this becomes a great model. If they are not, it becomes a difficult road to travel.

3. Set appropriate expectations from what your franchisees are expected to do and what you will do for them, right from the beginning. Setting the appropriate culture for how we interact with the brand should be unyielding, and strongly committed to right from the beginning

STEVE HANSEN

Over the last 30-plus years, Steve has dedicated himself to directly impacting the franchising industry in Australia. He has worked at all possible levels of franchise management.

Steve was the founder, Chief Chook, Managing Director, and Owner of the CHOOKS fresh & tasty restaurant business, Steve built the system up to over 40 stores before the selling the business in 2010.

Steve has been a franchisee, franchisor, franchise consultant, and a key driver of franchising in Australia through his roles as an FCA State Committee member, State President, and Board Member. He has and continues to go far beyond the ordinary expectations or demands of a group member.

He is now a partner and management consultant with Think DONE Management Consultancy. Think DONE consults to many varying businesses including, franchisors, master franchisees, franchisees, and all business owners in Western Australia.

Steve is completely passionate about franchising, with a Diploma in Business (Franchising), and holding the position of President of the WA Chapter of the Franchise Council of Australia from 2003-2008. Steve is a recipient of the Paddy Thompson Contribution to Franchising Award in 2007. He continues to assist the industry through the FCA WA Chapter committee.

Steve is a champion bloke, outstanding business leader, and franchising expert, and his sole purpose in life is to help others in business.

Q. Why should business owners think and behave like a franchisor?

Because most Franchisors understand that business is a journey, and in order to grow a brand, the many pieces of the jigsaw must be put together and be presented to a franchisee so that they are able to follow the system.

A franchisor or any business owner should provide hope and vision in a positive manner and always focus on the reputation of the brand.

The franchisor/business owner must always take decisions which will be good for ALL parties, and dismiss individual agendas that are not aligned with the brand.

The franchisor/business owner should understand the overall strategy and know that the 10 areas of any good business plan are all aligned. The franchisor/business owner must know WHY there is a culture within the business or NOT.

Q. What lessons did you learn from franchising?

Many. Making every mistake possible ensures that one learns, but it is about not making the same mistakes over and over. Not taking advice from qualified consultants, accountants, and lawyers was the difference between having 40 outlets and 400 over a period of 15 years. I spent 17 years not taking advice, spinning around in circles, building stores but not the people, and continued to make mistakes.

Organisation in the true sense starting with an organising board, showing every function of the business, then segregating so that it could be seen who sat where, and then putting the right people in the right seats, enabled a strong start in the right direction. Next came real statistics, weekly, and although we had been strong in this area over many years, we had not focused on the actual statistics which were the business drivers. So, by doing so and putting into graph form weekly, it was easy to see where the issues were. More importantly, it provided the accountability by the team and their responsibility lifted dramatically, which developed a great fun and competitive culture.

They learnt that there were only four questions to be covered every week as the agenda.

1. The financial management reporting.
2. A one page dashboard was the next imperative, as the business needed to be run to its financial model, and not from accounting and bookkeeping records, which in many cases are not available as required.
3. Business communications needed to be in place with simple systems for transfer of information, e.g. rosters, invoices, creditors, and debtors, so that communications flowed to the correct person within the company without being by passed, or any particular role being undermined.
4. Lastly, manuals and [procedures had to be documented in an easily read and accessible manner, so that franchisees and team members could have access as needed.

Q. What are your top three pieces of advice for business owners?

1. Work yourself out of a job, so that you can work on the business as a true executive.
2. Learn how to follow an organisation structure, which will enable growth, with great people which to whom you delegate all roles/functions, which you are not

good at. Make sure you have a strong long term plan that covers the 10 areas necessary and review this document, alongside your organisation board minimally every 6 weeks.

3. Have the discipline to run the business weekly in every respect.

Q. What are your top three pieces of advice for aspiring franchisors?

1. Seek advice from suitably qualified people who have real knowledge and experience in your business.
2. Build the financial model for a franchisee first, and always ensure that the profitability of franchisees is as imperative as shareholder of franchisor returns.
3. Build a financial model for the franchisor and follow the advice above for business owners.

Q. Any other business advice you would like to share?

Set BIG Goals. Determine the real Purpose of the business, and understand your own personal purpose—the WHY you get out of bed every day.

Understand that the only person that ever stops anything from happening is YOU.

Never throw out any ideas, but collect them and document, as tomorrow or next week or next year they just may be something great. Most ideas come from the people doing the work, and are looking for solutions to make it easier, so innovation and change will always be necessary.

PETER ELLIGETT

I first met Peter Elligett when I was 16 years old, and Peter was one of the managers I had at McDonald's. Peter was 'fast tracked' through the McDonald's system as a standout executive. After seven years with McDonald's, Peter finished up as a franchise consultant and had an initial national role with franchisor Cookie Man before purchasing his own franchise business in home services. He then got the opportunity to buy the Cookie Man business, and for the next 11 years, he owned and operated the business in Australia and expanded the brand into India.

His business was acquired by private equity, and he joined Allied Brands, who had acquired the Cookie Man brand as an executive director. The brand was merged with Mrs Fields bakery café in 2010, and Peter is now the CEO of the parent company for Mrs Fields, Cookies Australia.

As you can see from his history, Peter has held every possible role within the franchise sector, management, franchise consultant, franchisee, franchisor, general manager, director, and international franchisor. He has had private equity acquisition experience and been business owner. If it's happened in franchising, Peter has seen it, so he is well credentialed to share his thoughts and experiences on franchising and business ownership.

Q. Why would all business owners benefit from thinking like a franchisor?

Many businesses would benefit by adopting the principles of franchising. Whether or not a concept is franchisable, a business has a greater chance of success by breaking down each aspect and task within the business, and systemising, documenting, training, and coaching to ensure that everyone in the company can competently perform their role and has measurable performance targets. This is not confined to franchising, however. It's just that franchisors understand that they can only replicate success by using a systemised approach to the way they conduct their business.

Lessons from Franchising

I know that in the current climate, the following comments may be seen as glib, but as a responsible franchisor you have to have a proven, successful concept and look at every aspect of the business system. This ensures that you can provide the tools that will make the franchisees ultimately successful, profitable, expandable, and with the ability to have a great work/life balance. Following these principles, and not compromising on franchisee recruitment criteria or operational excellence, will put any franchisor on the path to success. In my own personal experience, when I have deviated or compromised on these core principles, whether due to economic or industry circumstances, the business has suffered accordingly. Having gone through the McDonald's management system over many years, I can honestly say that I use many of the competencies and principles that I learned there on a daily basis. The structure and systematic approach is still my benchmark in franchising today.

Advice to New Business Owners

1. Understand what your personal and company vision and values are, and make decisions that align with those principles.
2. Put together the best team possible and surround yourself with individuals that share your dream. Objectively identify your weaknesses, and hire people who can excel in the competencies that you don't have.
3. Delegate roles and responsibilities to your team—you can't do it all yourself. Owner burnout is often the catalyst for failure in what could be, and should be, a highly successful businesses or concept.

Advice to Aspiring Franchisors

1. Prove the concept in multiple company outlets before you contemplate franchising. The idea that you can expand an unproven business using franchisees money is seriously flawed no matter how many consultants tell you otherwise. Investigate rolling the concept with company owned outlets or the other quasi franchise models such as joint ownership (company/franchisee), which may require more capital, but give more control and ultimately higher profitability.
2. Talk to as many franchisors as you can and get professional assistance documenting systems, operations manuals, etc. A group of mentors or advisory board including experienced franchisors, financial advisors, private equity, or potential investors will help you avoid some of the more costly mistakes and help you up the curve faster.
3. Get the franchisee recruitment right—from the start.
4. Know what your exit strategy is and set your business up accordingly.

THREE OF MY FRANCHISE READY CLIENTS

I want to share four examples and three case studies of clients who I have helped get 'franchise ready'.

The reason I have chosen these four businesses, is because they represent four different approaches to growth and the business formats that they have used to grow.

Chargrill Charlies

Chargrill Charlies started in 1989 and has 11 stores in Sydney with more on the way. The food is as good as you will get in the takeaway space, and they are a family-run business whose philosophy has always been, "If you take care of the customer, everything else will take care of itself."

Chargrill Charlie's uses a franchise model and has some 100% franchisee operated stores, but their preferred model is a 50/50 franchise partnership with their franchisees, where each party has a 50% investment. They run the business like a franchise and have a franchise agreement in place, but they share the risk and the upside, and operate as a true partnership.

This gives them more control than a standard franchise agreement and demonstrates to their franchise partners that it is a true partnership. Many franchise systems refer to their franchisees as partners, but Chargrill Charlie's actually lives this philosophy.

ANKUR SEHGAL
WOK ON INN & P'NUT NOODLE BARS

I have known Ankur Sehgal since 2013, when I started working with him in his business Wok on Inn. Back then he had acquired an established Asian style noodle chain and was operating four restaurants. The concept had been operating for over 10 years and hadn't had any updates to the original concept since its inception.

Ankur had gained extensive hospitality experience working in management for Outback Steakhouse in America, while studying at the prestigious Cornell university. After receiving his degree, he spent three years as an analyst with Voyager Capital.

When he came to Australia, he became a multi-site franchisee with Subway before acquiring the Wok on Inn Brand.

Ankur recognised the need to revamp every aspect of the Wok on Inn brand and has totally reinvented the business. Ankur is a student of business and studies the best retail businesses in the world with the view of emulating many of their aspects.

When Ankur engaged me, it was to assist with systemising his business and making it more profitable. He revamped the menu, redesigned the store designs, fit out and refurbished all stores, and engaged professional agencies to assist with all aspects of the brand.

My role was to get his business franchise ready by documenting every aspect of the operations and creating the tools and resources he needed to be a world class operation.

Ankur never wanted to be the biggest restaurant brand in Australia in the Asian fast casual dining space—he wanted to be the best.

Fast forward five years, and he is well on his way to achieving his dream, but the next step is to actually franchise the operation.

Ankur has 12 restaurants today, and all are company owned and operated, with the average sales of the restaurants have increased by over 150% and total sales have grown by over 500%.

Ankur has been ready to franchise his business for the past four years, but has made the conscious decision to not franchise until he is 100% happy that his franchisees can achieve a level of profit and return on investment that he himself would be happy with.

Ankur has adopted a management equity program for his key management team, where he offers a percentage buy in for each restaurant and does so at attractive rates, with further options for his team to acquire a greater percentage stake in the business over time.

At this stage, we are looking to become a franchisor and grant franchises in 2020.

Q. Why should business owners think and behave like a franchisor?

The statistics for failure rate of small businesses are very high. Most people who get into business have a great idea or product or service. However, having that idea or skills or product does not necessarily ensure success.

Once we start a business, we are not the only person doing the work. All of a sudden we are wearing multiple hats—CEO, CFO, CIO, CMO, etc. We may be the best barista, but how do we ensure that everyone else makes coffee like us?

The solution is to start the business as a franchise, whereby we systemise everything. This is what a franchise is—a franchisor develops a system/brand etc., that different franchisees can operate and ensure consistency throughout the world. They key word here is 'system'. If every business has a system, the founder can remove or replace themselves from the business, or do a particular job, and the business will continue to thrive. The system manages the people, and the people keep improving the system.

Q. What lessons did you learn from franchising?

A lot—the importance of capital, controls, and customers. We call them my three Cs. A lot of businesses are not successful, because they do not structure correctly from a capital and controls perspective, or anticipate future capital needs. And the #1 thing are your customers: both internal and external. Your internal customers drive your business, and without external ones there is no business.

Q. *What are your top three pieces of advice for business owners?*

Have a vision—whether you want to set up a small café or the next airline, every business needs to have something greater than just making a profit. It drives the founder, your people, and even customers and suppliers. Apart from the vision, have a plan but know that plans can change, so develop a vision that's greater than yourself.

Fall in love with your people, not products or services—most business owners love their product or service so much that they forget their people. It is a recipe for failure, as people come first.

Take care of yourself—this is very important, as between serving customers, paying suppliers, and running a business, we forget to take care of us—the founder. Find and grow your own talents, and delegate the rest. You should not be a jack-of-all-trades, but rather a leader who provides a clear vision. This will help you stay in love with what you do!

Q. *What are your top three pieces of advice for aspiring franchisors?*

Your #1 stakeholder is the franchisee—in between the shareholders, directors, customers, and suppliers most franchisors forget the person who is driving our business—the franchisee. A franchisee who is a raving fan can lead to exponential goal, and a disgruntled franchisee can destroy your business.

Growth isn't everything—this is a hard one, but the history of franchising is full of companies that have taken on too much and then spend years or decades rectifying that. A business needs to grow, but the growth needs to be supported. That can mean the difference between a flash in the pan and a lasting success.

Stay ahead of the competition—anticipating and continuously investing in today and tomorrow is the name of the game. Most businesses are so agile when they start, and then forget all the rules that made them successful. Before long, a new competitor follows the same beginner's rule book of agility, anticipation, and passion, then beats us at our own game.

WADE DEATH
JACK & CO CONVENIENCE STORES

I started working with Wade in 2016, and in 2017 we started getting the business even more franchise ready than it already was, by documenting the systems and putting together all the materials Wade would need to franchise his business.

Wade had a distinguished corporate career as a senior manager with Caltex over eight years, and identified an opportunity to revolutionise the petrol and convenience sector. And in 2012, he created his own business in that sector with the establishment of his chain Jack & Co.

Wade has been a board member (board president 2017/2018) For the Australasian Convenience & Petroleum Marketers Association (ACAPMA), and his business has won numerous industry awards.

Wade had turned the sector on its head. Traditionally, petrol is the lead product offering for the petrol and convenience sector, with 80% of sales coming from fuel and 20% from convenience purchases. Jack & Co is the exact opposite with 80% of the business coming from store transactions. The changes we're seeing in this sector have been pioneered by Wade and his team.

Wade had resisted the temptation to venture into franchising, as the petrol and convenience sector has had a terrible reputation as a franchise operation. Wade is franchise ready, but has taken on a hybrid model of company stores with an operating partner that adheres to all the same principles and requirements of a franchisee and franchise operation.

General Comments on Franchising

I've been around franchise systems for most of my working life, and am fortunate to have seen the very large and the very small. In many respects, the word 'franchise' scares people … It certainly scared me. In recent years, we've seen countless scandals where franchisees have cut corners to make the model work (and I guess in some cases, the model probably worked but they've been greedy). If you strip franchising back to how it all began, it's about having someone else operate your brand. Generally, the principles are always pretty consistent—there's a branded marketing system and some operational system that you buy into (in various forms), and you are supported by the creator of the system to make it work. Being able to break down your business into these 'systems' is an outstanding discipline to be in no matter what your intentions are.

My business has been around for over six years now, and we've only been franchising for the last year. During that time, I had countless offers to franchise and countless people tell me I was mad not to franchise,… but ultimately, I consider someone else investing in your business as the greatest privilege of all. Equally, in my mind it heightens the stakes considerably to make sure you get it right, for you and for them.

Q. What lessons did you learn from franchising?

I've not long ago gone down this path (I resisted for some time!) and would claim I have just as many lessons from 'not franchising' as I do from franchising. My business, like most, took some time to develop its offer and refine the model, so I personally didn't want to have to 'negotiate' these changes through franchisees along the way. With a company operated network, we could adapt the model quickly and make decisions on behalf of our store operations without consultation, in that sense I think, somewhat ironically, we got ready to franchise quicker by not franchising. During this time, we made bucket loads of decisions ... Some of them worked, and some of them didn't, but I always knew for every wrong decision and every wrong turn, I was closer to the right one!

Like all small and growing businesses, we hit a point of plateau and decided what we wanted to be famous for ... developing the system or operating the system. I believed we couldn't do both (I admire those who can!), and the more conversations I had with interested parties, the more I realised how much passion other people had for our business too. It's probably been my most pleasing and rewarding aspect of the journey so far, to see people come out of nowhere and be absolute disciples of the brand and business I set out to create. It's enormously flattering. So, what were my lessons? Recruit passion but make sure you can back it up with rigour, discipline, and a solid business model.

Q. Why should business owners think and behave like a franchisor?

I would go so far as to say some of the best franchise businesses in the world are the most disciplined. It's incredibly rare that a business can survive without discipline—even creative agencies are known for discipline around how they approach a problem, how they challenge themselves for the right outcomes, and how they ensure they deliver for the client.

I know when I reflect on my adventure thus far, I think of the point at which I first had people invest their hard earned money in my business. I didn't sleep at night when it was in my Account! I kept thinking of the incredible obligation I had to ensure I always delivered. And as time has marches on, I generally find that what gets our licensees through time and time again are the disciplines that our model provides. We need to be creative in our marketing, our branding, and our consumer proposition, but when it comes to operating the business, we need disciplines. Whether you're franchising or not, try and run a business without discipline and you'll fail. Generally speaking, we're not only developing some rigour in our operations, but we're reminding our licensees of their obligations as employers and operators of their business. And yes, they're quick to remind us of things too! I think everyone should get themselves into that headspace as soon as possible, whether you're actually franchising or not.

Q. What are your top three pieces of advice for business owners?

Surround yourself with the best people. I used to work for a guy who always said 'First who, then what'. Time and time again, I remind myself (sometimes the hard way) that it's not people who make the difference —it's good people who make the difference.

What's your lasting point of difference? Your point of difference is what people talk about, it's what they look for and, it's what they cross to the other side of the street for (in consumer facing businesses of course). We tend to get caught up in the operations, the tactics, the bits and pieces, the reports, and the analysis (I know I do), but ultimately few businesses survive without a lasting point of difference. I frequently try to remind myself of that.

When you're nailing it, beware, others are watching closer than you think. When you're on fire people take note and they have every chance to look at you … but you don't have the same chance to look at them until their offer is in the market. The old saying goes, it's easier to get to number one than it is to stay there … and yes, that's probably what keeps me awake at night more than anything!

Q. What are your top three pieces of advice for aspiring franchisors?

Don't franchise for money's sake. Personally, I don't buy that franchising should be your source of funds for growth. It helps, of course, but your business needs to be on its own two feet before you take someone else's money to operate it. Franchisees should be a turbo charger, not a bank (but countless people would disagree with me on that).

When you decide you're going to franchise, you're probably still a year away. I say to people starting a business is like going on holidays … you need twice as much money and twice as much time as you think! When we really decided we wanted to work on our systems, there was a big lead time involved to be really ready, but equally, some things you can only get on top of when you have franchisees in your business!

Be selective. And don't apologise for that.

Q. Any other business advice you would like to share?

Two things:

1. Solve a problem—In this instance I mean a market problem, but you could apply that to many things. I am constantly reminded that just by surviving we are bucking the statistics of new businesses (which are horrifying … I try not to think about it), but I also think in some instances, businesses are created with a great product that doesn't really fit a market need. I think our business was fortunate to grow quickly because the market response was so significant.

2. Play to your strengths—when you're in business you get lots of feedback—lots! It's probably something I found the hardest, and when it's your business you always take it personally. What I found throughout this is that the expectation on me as the founder of the business was to be an expert on everything, and yet the silly thing is that if it wasn't your business there wouldn't be the same expectation on you. For years, I worked hard to build up a team around me to counter my weaknesses (and they tell me I have many), and honestly I think that's when it started to fall into place for me. We have hundreds of staff, millions of dollars going through the company, and 1.4m customers per annum, and trying to be an expert in everything would have crippled the business.

PETE HASELHURST
—MILKY LANE BURGER BARS

I met Pete in 2017 when I was asked by a lawyer who was looking to act for Pete in his business called Milky Lane, a burger Restaurant in Bondi NSW that infuses the love of music with the love of food. Milky Lane offers a wide variety of burgers, desserts, and cocktails in a modern and hip setting.

Pete is a passionate and driven entrepreneur, whose big ideas have lead him to achieve an impressive business portfolio.

In 2011 with over ten years' experience working in various promotional, marketing, and sales roles, Pete decided to venture out on his own, establishing his first business. With great success in that business and a strong entrepreneurial spirit, he has expanded his business portfolio and is now invested in over 12 businesses.

The majority of his businesses are independent, but he also operates six franchised businesses as a franchisee, so he understands franchising from both a franchisee's and franchisor's perspective.

I have been working with Pete and his team at Milky Lane since 2017, and have gotten them ready to franchise their Milky Lane business. From one store in early 2018, we now have more than 10 stores operating through a franchise model in Australia, and the business has grown by over 300% in 2018 and will double again in 2019 and again in 2020.

Pete shares with us his experiences as a franchisor and how different it is to being an independent business owner or franchisee.

Q. Why should business owners think and behave like a franchisor?

There is no better way to grow and scale a business than to create and implement systems that work. Systems allow your business to operate without you being there, and that's what business is all about.

A franchise business is the pinnacle of business 'systems', you're simply in the business of selling systems that work. You find yourself selling two separate products, at Milky Lane, we started selling burgers, cocktails, and desserts and then progressed to selling burgers, cocktails, desserts, and systems.

If you document and systemise every successful action within your business, you will eventually have a systemised business that operates and has the potential to scale with reduced labour and minimal room for error.

Regardless of whether or not you want to create a franchise business—creating a business that has a systemised and structured approach to everything will increase your probability of being successful.

What lessons did you learn from franchising?

1. Be franchise ready. Make sure your systems and products are ready to franchise, if they are then your life as a franchisor will be far more productive. Franchisees rely on your product and systems to make money, and it's your responsibility to ensure that you're ready in order for them to operate a profitable business when following your systems. Franchisees

will ask less questions and you can spend your time working on improving and growing the business.

2.   Slow down. Choose your franchisees very carefully and don't just take the first person who is interested. It's easy to get excited and say 'yes' to the first application, but understand that there will be times when the relationship gets tough, and you need to have a franchisee who respects your business and understands what it takes to be successful.

3.   Have skin in the game. If your franchisee doesn't have money or security on the line, then pass the opportunity. If they have nothing to lose, they will have nothing to stay for when hurdles arise. Your aim is to have a franchisee with business experience and a level of security or cash in the bank.

4.   Are you an owner operator? Your franchisee must be an owner operator, otherwise they will employ someone who doesn't care, and the franchisee will blame the franchisor for a system that doesn't work.

5.   Train the trainer. Train your franchisees to a level where they can train the founder of the franchise. The training will be the key to your success. The more time you spend on training, the more successful your franchise model will be.

6.   Get the right agreement. Your franchise agreement controls your franchisee, ensure you have a tight agreement that allows you to control your franchise operation. There will be times when you need to refer to your agreement and ensuring that you have every corner covered will give you full control over your franchise business.

Q. *What are your top three pieces of advice for business owners?*

1.   Every cent matters. A business operates on making money, so understand exactly where every cent of your revenue and expenses are. Ensure that you have daily, weekly and, monthly accounts.

2.   Don't be emotional. You will be faced with daily choices and decisions, some will be tougher than others, but ultimately your business success is based on making the right choices and each of the decisions that you make. Remove emotions, and make a decision based on facts, data, and what's best for the brand.

3.   Know your customer. Understand the importance of knowing who your customer is and what their habits are. You want your customers to LOVE what you do. Allocate time to communicate with your customers and audience throughout your social media channels, because without a customer you don't have a business.

Q. *What are your top three pieces of advice for aspiring franchisors?*

1.   Get your numbers right first. Before you sell a franchise, understand the importance of getting your numbers right. Know what your industry margins are and get your numbers inline to ensure your franchise model will be a success.

2.   Do your homework. Know your competitors, study your market, and communicate with your audience. The more

information you know, the more chance you have of making the right decision. Every decision you make will have an effect on your business

3.   Take your time. You have one chance to launch your franchise model, so if you're not ready then take your time to get it right. Your first five franchises are the key to your success, so get them right and your journey will be more successful.

Q. Any other business advice you would like to share.

1.   Make sure you love what you do, because times will get tough. If you don't love what you do, you will resent the business, and may have a failed business with debt and a failure on your resume.

2.   Don't re-mortgage the house to get into business. The world we live in today has changed, and the cost to open a business or test a concept is minimal compared to what it was 15 years ago.

3.   Enjoy the journey, don't focus on money as the only goal, and understand that business isn't easy, because if it was everyone would have a successful business.

4.   Have fun, look smart, and always remember why you got into it.

FLIPPING OUT

CHAPTER 12

SO YOU WANT TO START A FRANCHISE

Step-by-Step Process

"You can't do well unless your franchisees do well."

—**Richard Cole, Founder of Geeks on Call**

WHY WOULD YOU WANT TO FRANCHISE?

I have to admit, I am a massive advocate for franchising and as such, I think the 'How' is actually the easy part of the equation. Easy in the sense that there is a methodology to how to do it, assuming that the business is in fact franchisable. I have had to turn away potential franchisors when I didn't believe that it could be, or should, be franchised.

The more difficult or salient issue is the 'why'. Why the prospective franchisor wants to franchise, and if there is a good reason to do it, and it makes sense, then the 'how' is easy.

The first question I ask any prospective franchisor is 'why' they want to franchise, and this question enables me to determine if they have thought through the idea of franchising, and whether they should or not. Don't get me wrong, some people have not thought through all of the aspects associated with becoming a franchisor, so I take them on a journey to make sure they are aware of what to expect and why they should or shouldn't franchise.

Interestingly, I was with a franchise lawyer recently with three of my new clients, and they were taking us through the options that should be considered before setting their sights on becoming a franchisor. This lawyer outlined the choices in broad terms and offered the opportunity to conduct a workshop to flesh out which way the clients should go. The options they offered up were—franchise, license, and partnership or company operations with investors. All of these were options I hadn't had extensive experience with the licensed model, so it was good to hear about the other options and to weigh them up and to get a different perspective. I thought it was pretty clear that all three of these businesses should become franchises, and that is how we have proceeded, but the process was worthwhile and I encourage prospective franchisors to get at least two perspectives.

The most common reasons that a business should consider franchising are:

- Not having the capital to grow through a corporate structure.
- Using franchisee's capital to open and grow the business making it cheaper to grow.
- Less direct human resource management than operating all locations yourself.
- The ability to scale the business faster.
- The ability to grow in remote markets from the original locations and head office.
- The premise of franchising is that an owner will do a better job than an employee, as they have 'skin in the game'. The key to this is recruiting the right franchisees.
- 'Passactive' income through royalties.
- Opportunity for product rebates and proprietary product margin.
- The opportunity to take your business international.

Considerations for Franchising

Make sure the business model is working and that you can demonstrate that it has worked for a period of time. There's no set or minimum time frame or legislation to comply with, nor currently any requirements that a franchisor demonstrate competence, but there's a certain number of practical considerations.

A client of mine, Lukumades, came to me in 2017 with only two prototype operations, a retail store, a food truck, and a bit less than one year of trading. We broke each component of the business down and looked at the business model for both operations, and determined that although the business originated from the operations of a food truck, that part of the model was not sustainable nor franchisable. When we first met the business model needed tweaking, sales needed to grow, and profitability needed to improve. With tweaks to the model and a concerted marketing and sales strategy, the business sales doubled, and the profitability was on par with the best food franchises in Australia. After 12 months of concerted focus and working together, the model was ready to franchise, and very quickly we were able to roll out five stores in the first year of franchising.

It's one thing to want to roll out a franchise model and to have a business that makes sense to franchise, but the business model also needs to be attractive to potential franchisees. While it is difficult to quantify 'salability', factors such as credibility, uniqueness, and brand 'X-Factor' all contribute. Though a young business, the Lukumades management team had good credibility, and the concept was clearly differentiated in the market. Moreover, they already had a handful of unsolicited franchise inquiries—always a good sign when it comes to salability. I am a strong believer that if enough people ask you if you're a franchise, then you should consider whether you can, or should, franchise.

The key to success in franchising is making sure that your business is easy to replicate. If the concept only works because of a unique location, a superstar salesperson, or because an owner is working 80-hour weeks, it is going to be difficult to replicate. Ideally, a franchise concept should be relatively simple to operate, and should be able to work in a variety of markets. Of course, potential franchisees can certainly bring some previous experience, some special skills, or qualifications to the table. In the case of Lukumades, the owner is the most extroverted business owner who you could meet. From serenading customers on the street in front of his store to dancing like no one is watching, his charisma is infectious to the point that he makes even the most reserved person extroverted. His name is Ex, and we like to say he has the 'X' factor. What we needed to do is make sure that his business model also had the 'X' factor; that it has personality, but it also had to be easily teachable and readily duplicated.

Profitability is the key, not just for the franchisee, but also for the franchisor, and that is why the opportunity needs to be modelled to make sure all parties can make a fair return. If it doesn't work for both parties, then it should not be franchised.

A franchisee who is an owner-operator will expect to get a return, both for the time that they spend in the business, as well as their investment in the franchise. With Lukumades, the simplicity of the business model, which resulted in lower than industry average labour costs, the low cost of goods, and the locations primarily focused on high streets and away from shopping centres, meant significantly lower occupancy costs, enabling the profitability to be the best I know of within the food sector, and the return on investment achieved between 1-2 years of operation.

Just as important is the franchisors ability to generate a fair return on their time and investment in getting the business to the point of franchising. Setting up a franchise system is not cheap, so you need to make sure the franchisor can get a fair return. In the early stages of the franchisor's business, the franchisor will not make much money and will most certainly pay themselves less than they have ever been paid before, but franchising for a franchisor is about the long term return and building equity in the asset.

I wrote earlier about value, and in franchising, relationships are critical. The most successful franchisors are typically those that are the most committed to making sure that their franchisees are successful, and that they receive value for their initial investment and their ongoing contribution to using the IP of the brand (royalties).

While one of the reasons to become a franchisor is to utilise the capital of others, and franchising may be seen as a low-cost means of expansion, it is not a 'no cost' strategy. A new franchisor will need capital to develop legal documents, manuals, training programs, and marketing materials, not to mention a marketing budget for franchise lead generation. It has been estimated that the average cost of attracting a franchisee can be as much as $20,000, and it can take as many as 100 leads to convert one franchisee, and the overall cost of setting up a franchisor business can range between $70,000 to $200,000 without factoring in the owner's/founder's time.

Common Mistakes

Underestimating Costs

While franchising can make your company (and you) wildly successful, it can also sink you into a massive hole if you don't have enough money from the outset.

Being undercapitalised really inhibits growth for both the franchisor and the franchisee. Every time I have seen a problem in franchising it typically relates to cashflow and profitability. As a new franchisor, there is very little cash flow.

You really don't make money on the sale of a franchise. This influx of funds is pretty much chewed up by the cost to recruit, launch, and support your new franchisee. You make your money based on the ongoing royalties. In the early stages with only a few franchisees, you will spend more money supporting your franchisees than you will make from the royalties, so a good way to fund your operation is to continue running profitable, company run operations.

Overestimating Returns

Business owners by their very nature are optimistic, and if you've been ballsy enough to start a franchise business model, you are typically entrepreneurial. One of their key character traits is optimism. I always advise franchisors and franchisees to be conservative with their projections of sales, and overzealous in their projection of costs; to always complete a minimum of three scenarios when determining the budget and cashflow of the business. Complete a low, medium, and high forecast and base all your decisions on worst case scenario. If you can't make it work at that level, then you need to go back and tweak the business model or even reconsider whether you franchise or not.

The McDonald's Example

Ray Kroc opened his first McDonald's in April 1955 in the Chicago suburb of des Plaines. He created a flagship store as a showcase for selling McDonald's franchises to the rest of the country. For each franchise he sold, Ray would collect 1.9% of the gross sales. From that, he would give the McDonalds 0.5%. Kroc sold 18 franchises in his first year in franchising the business, but he was shocked to discover he was barely making enough money to cover his expenses. In his haste to acquire the rights to the McDonalds' methods, he had made them a deal they couldn't refuse. Unfortunately, it was a deal on which he couldn't make any money.

If you've seen the movie *The Founder*, you'll know that he 'renegotiated a better deal' so that the model could be profitable.

He also changed his approach around the property and began to buy the land and lease it back to the franchisee, generating rental income. Today, McDonald's owns more real estate than anyone, and generates a significant portion of their profitability from the rental margin of the restaurants they operate and lease back to the franchisee.

Had Ray Kroc completed better financial modelling, he may have negotiated a better deal up front, but the reality, is you always need to be looking at your business model to make sure it's working the best for everyone.

What Business Are You In?

All franchisors start out as business owners and perfect their model, and for those that choose a franchise route, it is important to make the distinction between the change in roles and requirements as you become a franchisor. A business owner only has to focus on one business and the operations of it, while the skill set and requirements of a franchisor are significantly different.

Being a franchisor is a different business altogether, and although I recommend franchisors maintain company operations, you need to have different resources looking after each operation. The best systems recognise the different skills required to **manage** a company operation and **lead** a franchisee. Working with franchisees is much more of a consultative process, as you have to influence the franchise business owner. You cannot just tell them what to do.

Many franchisors venture into vertical integration as a way of managing the supply chain for both quality and financial reasons, but it is important to know what business you are in. If you are to diversify, you need to make sure that you have dedicated and specialised resources to manage different divisions within the business.

I have first-hand experience as the CEO of a retail franchised food chain. We operated three businesses, a retail chain, a franchise model, and a manufacturing division, thinking we could control quality and generate a financial return from three different income sources. The problem was, we overcomplicated the business model and were not specialists in all three divisions. This saw a significant loss from our manufacturing business, which directly impacted the profitability and continued viability of the overall business.

There are franchisors who do this well by contract manufacturing their proprietary products and leaving the production to manufacturers who specialise in that product, and have better efficiencies and volumes. If you're looking for additional income, consider product supply through contract manufacturers, but make sure that your franchisees are still getting a great deal; better than they could get anywhere else.

The Franchise Consultant

There are a lot of 'franchise experts' to choose from. Some market better than others and some are better than others. I have done a lot of work in this space in the past couple of years, and all of my work is referrals from happy clients. I am often gob smacked by the lack of quality in this space, and some of the consultants that charge way too much for what they do.

My firm recommendation for aspiring franchisors is to make sure they talk to experienced franchise consultants; individuals who have broad experience in that they have been through a range of roles and seniority within a franchise business, and that their experience is current. You don't want someone who's been sitting in an office for 10 years—you want someone who knows about modern day franchising. The bigger franchise consulting firms have a broader range of services and experiences, but also have a lot of non-franchising people working for them. Make sure the consulting group you decide on have relevant and current experience.

If possible, make sure they know your industry and have good testimonials from other franchisors. Finally, shop around and get three quotes so you know what you're getting, with whom you'll be working, and whether they will do a piece of the work or take the whole journey with you.

Some consultants will do the strategy and create the documentation, while others are full service and can help you with every aspect of going to market.

There is a list of services that a good franchise consulting firm should offer as part of their package, and what an emerging franchisor needs and this includes the following:

1. **An initial strategy session that includes the following:**
    - A review of the potential market and mapping of the size of the opportunity.
    - A high level review of the financial model and evaluation for the franchisor and franchisee.
    - An investment analysis.
    - A review of the required resources.
    - What human resources will be needed and what can be outsourced.
    - Creation of a sales process for franchising
    - A recommendation of law firm and strategy session with a franchise lawyer.
    - A review of all existing materials like operations and training manuals, materials, and IP.
    - Recommendation of franchise fees and royalties.
    - Outline of franchise sales process and recommended activities.
    - Recommendations on required training for franchisees.
    - Advice on accounting structure
    - A summary report which details the next steps, and a list of recommendations including what services may be required and a quotation of those services.

How— Step-by-Step Process

It's important to understand what costs the emerging franchisor will be faced with. The franchise strategy session will determine if franchising is in fact the right model to assist growing the business and helping to achieve the founders/business owners goals.

The costs associated with establishing a franchise is typically the following:

Feasibility study	$7,000	– $30,0000
Accounting and structuring	$8,000	– $15,000
Franchise documentation	$10,000	– $35,000
General legal advice and trade mark protection	$5,000	– $10,000
Operations & Training manual	$10,000	– $30,000
Marketing	$10,000	– $30,000
Advertising	$15,000	– $30,000
Sales program	$5,000	– $20,000
Total	**$70,000**	**– $200,000**

Depending on what the business the business already has in place, these costs may be reduced to a degree. You may recall in chapter 9, my recommendation is for the franchisor to always have three months of working capital in the bank. To determine, this you need to complete a costs forecast, budget, cash flow forecast, and break-even analysis.

The Legal Aspects

Selecting the right lawyer is critical, and the franchise consultant should help you, and often a law firm may assist you find the right franchise consultant. I have three law firms that refer clients to me.

Make sure the law firm you use is a franchise specialist, and ideally, they have done another business within your sector or industry.

They will educate you on everything that you need to know, including the franchise code of conduct and what your obligations are as a franchisor. They will also help you and your franchise consultant determine if a franchise model is the right vehicle for you to pursue.

The lawyers will:
- Register trademarks.
- Register your intellectual property.
- Send you a questionnaire to be completed with your franchise consultant for the franchise agreement and the disclosure document.
- Advise you on the correct structure but this needs to be discussed with your accountant to ensure what the lawyer recommends is aligned to your personal and family circumstances.

A typical legal structure may look something like the diagram below, and will therefore require some additional entities to be created. This is done to protect you and your assets, but needs to be entered into after consultation with your accountant.

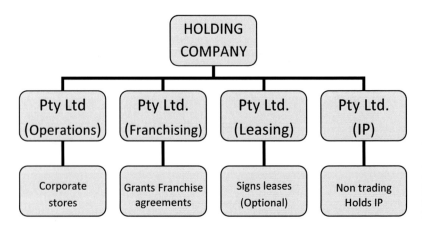

What Assets Will You Need to Create?

There are a number of assets that you will need to have in place, including:

1. Standard Operating Procedures
2. Operations Manual
3. Training Manual
4. Opening/Business set up Manual
5. Financial Model
6. Brand Guidelines
7. Legal Documents
8. Marketing Manual
9. Investor Packs
10. Leasing Pack
11. Compliance Guidelines

Standard Operating Procedures

Every aspect of your operations need to be documented into a step-by-step procedure that can be used to set the expected standards, train new team members, and verify proficiency of team members on an ongoing basis.

Operations Manual

Often referred to as the brand bible and often referenced in the franchise agreement. It's impossible, and not recommended to try, to include too much detail in the franchise agreement; it's best to reference the operations manual. The operations manual details the 'how-to' of every aspect of your business and includes both soft and hard skills, and acts as a troubleshooting guide for the business and management team.

Common chapters include:

Introduction—Explains how the operations manual works, the brand story and history including values, strategy, franchise relationship, and franchise management.

Policies & Procedures—A summary of all of the expected obligations of the team members in the business, including induction and all relevant policies like rosters, breaks, uniforms, phone use, drug alcohol policy, OHS requirements, leave, employee handbook, etc.

Product—Outlines the standards of all goods, services, and products that are used, made, and sold to customers. This section outlines the control standards that need to be met.

People—This is typically the most detailed aspect of the operations manual. You've heard me reference that we are all essentially in the people business. This chapter covers the following: employment practices, recruitment, induction, training, performance management, business standards, and all of the tools and resources used in managing the people resource in the business.

Safety & Security—As an employer, you have a duty of care to ensure that you provide a safe and secure working environment for your team.

Business Administration—This chapter addresses all the management functions from an administrative perspective, including cost control areas like cost of goods, wage cost control, controllable expense management, operational and financial audits, and any financial requirements. Essentially all of the administration requirements of the franchisor and best practice for the franchisee.

Leadership & Management—This chapter includes all of the soft skills needed by management to implement and manage the systems and people in the business.

Technical—Is the specific technical aspects of the trade.

Training Manual

The training manual is typically designed for the franchisee and management team, and is designed to introduce the new franchisee or manager to every aspect of the business. This manual directs them to complete all aspects of the business operations using a building block approach, and is designed to train a novice to become a proficient business leader.

Opening/Business Set Up Manual

This manual is a comprehensive checklist of every aspect of the physical establishment of a new franchise unit, and is usually broken down into activities that both the franchisee and franchisor need to complete. This has time frames attached to it, and is used to ensure every new business completed tasks in a timely manner, so it can open for business according to the agreed schedule.

Financial Model

This is designed to ensure that the business model can generate enough of a financial return for both the franchisee and the franchisor. This requires two different tools and will usually require someone strong in finance to create the tool. A good franchisor will provide a template for their franchisees to model scenarios. It's important that the franchisor not make any representations about expectations, but should provide actual results as a benchmark and the tool for the franchisee to evaluate the opportunity.

Brand Guidelines

It's extremely important that the franchisor have established marketing and brand guidelines that are consistent with the IP that is registered. These guidelines ensure consistency between franchise locations. All marketing collateral and use of the brand needs to be consistent as this is one of the benefits of a franchise brand.

Legal Documents

The law firm that you engage will assists you putting together all the legal aspects required of a franchisor. The franchise sector is governed and highly regulated, so getting the right legal advice is imperative.

Registration of your trademark and Intellectual property is essential to ensure that you limit the likelihood of someone copying yours or registering marks and preventing you from using them.

The law firm will assist you with advice relating to the way you structure your franchise, and this should be considered based on the professional accounting advice you receive regarding your personal circumstances.

You will need to create a franchise agreement and disclosure document, and your lawyer will help you with this. This is critical, because franchising is becoming extremely regulated around the world. In Australia, the franchising sector is overseen by the Trade Practices (Industry Codes—Franchising), which is a code of conduct, prescribed pursuant to the Competition and Consumer Act. The Australian Competition and Consumer Commission (ACCC) is the government agency responsible for promoting compliance with this code.

Marketing Manual

This manual is different from the brand guidelines, but utilises the brand standards documented in there. The marketing manual is like a toolbox of ideas and programs that can be used to run local marketing campaigns by the franchisee.

Investor Packs

This is a high quality piece of marketing collateral for prospective franchisees, and outlines the features and benefits of the franchise opportunity for prospective franchisees. It typically includes the following: The business history and philosophy, the products or services offered, how the opportunity is differentiated, the market and customers, the turn-key nature of the business including everything that the franchisor does in getting the business going, marketing, training, ongoing support, the commercial aspects of the opportunity, the steps in the recruitment process, and frequently asked questions. It is designed to provide more detail than is listed on the franchise website.

Leasing Pack

The leasing pack is designed for bricks and mortar businesses that require a physical premises, and is designed to show the landlord what to expect from the franchise business. This pack includes imagery, location designs, and information relating to the desired locations. These are used to help leasing agents source ideal locations, and for securing locations by impressing the landlords and property owners.

Compliance Guidelines

Every business, once they have established standards, needs to have a mechanism to measure compliance with the desired operational standards. These compliance checks are scored assessments of the business, are graded, and can be used to determine minimum operational standards and suitability for franchisee expandability or continuance within the business. They are also used to recognise outstanding performance and benchmarking standards.

Once Established

So, let's assume that you have been successful and gotten the business launched as a franchise model. I referenced earlier that the easy part of franchising is the creation of the tools and systems to get going. The harder part of being a franchisor is the ongoing leadership and management that you need to provide, to ensure a successful franchise system for you and your franchisees.

The key considerations for a franchisor are:

1. Customer Satisfaction

At the heart of any business is the customer proposition. While this may seem obvious, the best practice franchisors have a focus on the customer proposition that develops loyalty and keeps them coming back. There is an understanding that each customer is more than just one transaction, and that the 'lifetime value' of their customers is many multiples of the first transaction.

I really like the example of Howard Schulz, founder of Starbucks, articulated in his book, *Pour Your Heart Into It: How Starbucks Built a Company One Cup at a Time*. Starbucks sells over four billion cups of coffee every year. In this book, Schulz says although we serve millions of cups of coffee every day, they view it as selling one cup of coffee, millions of times, the principle being, every customer is special.

It is important for all franchisors, and business owners for that matter, to look at not just their (traditional) external customers (those who pay for the goods and services), but also the 'internal customers', your team members. It is important to serve your team so that they can serve your customers.

As a franchisor, I have always had the philosophy and saying, "If you're not serving a customer, serve someone who is." This is particularly relevant for your head office support team. Their role is to support your field teams and franchisees. They are the reason that their roles exist, so it's important that your support team understand and practice this principle.

2. Measurement

You can't improve what you don't measure, and for that reason, you need to have well defined key performance indicators (KPI's), bench-marking, and financial performance. Ray Kroc created systems of measurement at McDonald's where everything was measured, and that has contributed to the success of McDonald's. You don't need to measure everything like they did/do, but you do need to identify what are the key aspects of the business that will drive the performance of the business.

Ensure that you have a business plan, and so to do your franchisees. Ensure your financial systems are set up and a chart of accounts established for your franchises, so that you can benchmark. Use these benchmarks to drive performance of the network and assist you with presenting the financial performance of the business to prospective franchisees.

Most importantly, measure operational standards against agreed minimum standards. Many franchisors create competition and link this performance to recognition programs as a way of driving performance and rewarding excellence.

3. Compliance

Compliance to the established standards is critical. Standards are essential to ensure consistency across the group. The most common complaint of better franchisees is that the franchisor is soft on compliance, and is letting other franchisees operate poorly, which reflects badly on their franchise and ultimately its value. These better franchisees may exit the franchise and move to a network with consistent and professional compliance standards. The best franchise systems understand that the customer promise conveyed by advertising and marketing must be executed by their franchisees. A system is only as strong as the weakest franchisee and their operation. If a franchisee does something damaging, it doesn't just impact their business, but it has the potential to impact the whole brand, so strong compliance management by the franchisor is essential.

4. Field Support

Compliance is important, but any franchise is a partnership between the franchisor and the franchisee. The best franchise systems are focused on developing their franchisees, to become better business people through education rather than policing.

The role of the field support person is to partner with the franchisee, and to help them achieve their personal and business goals. The field support team member combines consulting with compliance, coaching, and partnering.

5. Marketing

Nothing builds a business like a commitment to building the brand, both nationally and locally. The franchisor focuses on building the brand through a well-developed strategy with a marketing plan and calendar of events, a strong online presence and digital marketing strategy, in store promotions, quality marketing collateral, and advertising. But marketing shouldn't stop there. Each franchisee needs to market at a local level and become part of their local community. The franchisor has the responsibility to provide the franchisees with the tools and support to execute at a local level.

Having a minimum marketing spend detailed in the franchise agreement ensures continued marketing and brand building.

6. Continual Innovation

Innovation is how the best franchises keep ahead of the pack. They realise that competitors will eventually copy the market leaders and understand that differentiation is important—not just in product but in every aspect of the business.

I have two clients that have experienced copycats. Jack & Co has innovated the petroleum and convenience store market and has in recent times seen competitors copy their design and attributes but what they can't copy is their innovation and execution at the store front. My other client is Lukumades (Greek Doughnuts) they only started operations 3 years ago and there are already three copycats doing what they do with similar store designs, name and product offering but none of them have the 'X' factor.

Both of these clients are always innovating and looking at how they can improve, as they innovate their competitors will copy but they will always be behind them.

One of my other clients, Milky Lane is a burger business and you could argue that sector is overdone. They have a number of points of differentiation, and one of these key elements is their innovation. They keep their core offering tight but always have new products in each category every month, and these products are cutting edge and on trend. They do this by seeing what is happening internationally, but also by reinventing old classics that have a nostalgic appeal to customers.

7. Supply Chain Management

The philosophy of McDonald's is that of a three legged stool with each leg dependent on the other. Those legs are, the franchisees, the McDonald's corporate team, and their suppliers. They have recognised the importance of the supplier and that all stakeholders need to get a fair return.

When franchisors start to treat their suppliers as strategic partners, they start to approach best-practice, not only in franchising but in business generally. By harnessing the know-how and experience of their suppliers, good franchisors find a willing partner in new product research and development, because suppliers understand that assisting customers to grow will result in increasing sales volumes.

Earlier in this chapter, I wrote about vertical integration as a good way to manage quality and to generate additional revenue for the franchisor and better pricing for the franchisees.

8. Communication

The success of every relationship is dependent on the quality of the communication, and this is even more evident in a franchise system. I often joke that it's harder to get out of a franchise system than it is to get out of a marriage these days.

The franchisor-franchisee relationship is the cornerstone of a successful franchise network. This communication process often starts with an open mind, and a willingness to listen and respond to franchisee concerns. The process of monitoring and responding to franchisee concerns is where great franchise networks excel. Effective field visits, regular franchisee meetings, franchise advisory councils, franchisee product development input, regional advertising committees, and annual conferences are all hallmarks of outstanding franchisors.

I am a strong believer that every issue can be resolved through effective communication and by sitting across the table from the other party.

The Right First steps

Just like we referenced in chapter eight, managing the people aspects of franchising is critical. It starts with recruiting the right franchisees, and making sure that you are granting the rights and not selling the opportunity. The prospective franchisees need to be the right fit for your business; they need to share the same values and be the right fit for the system. I am a strong advocate of profiling and there are many franchise specific profiling tools available to assist you understand your prospects. I have always held the belief that if a prospective franchise is difficult or behaves badly from the outset, then it will only get worse once they enter your system. There is often a temptation in the early stages of a franchise system to lower your ideal standards of a franchisee. Just remember most franchise agreements are for terms of between 5 to 10 years, and that's a long time to deal with someone who pushes your buttons.

When a franchisee applies for a franchise, they do so because they want the support and expertise of the franchisor and brand. If the recruitment and selection processes are professionally developed and executed, every franchisee will understand the standards expected, and the processes they need to follow in order to be successful.

Once they are in you need to ensure that your well-developed training materials and documentation are well explained and actually used to onboard, train and lead your franchise partners.

<u>Takeaways</u>

❖ Get a good franchise consultant to manage the process for and with you.

❖ Meet with three franchise consultants and lawyers and obtain three quotes.

❖ Develop a franchise strategy.

❖ Create the assets you need to help you market the opportunity.

❖ Establish compliance standards.

❖ Develop an operational plan.
